# A COMMUNITY
# OF LOVE

# A
# COMM**UNITY**
# of LOVE

JAN TAYLOR

THIS BOOK IS DEDICATED TO MAYBUG,
TERRY, ANN, MICHAEL, JILL, PHIL,
HELEN AND MOST IMPORTANTLY OF ALL,
TO THE GLORY OF GOD.

Published by Zaccmedia
www.zaccmedia.com
info@zaccmedia.com

Published May 2019
Copyright © 2019 Janice Taylor

ISBN: 978-1-911211-91-4

British Library Cataloguing-in-Publication Data.
A catalogue record for this book is available from the British Library.

# CONTENTS

Introduction   9

**PART 1:** THE FOUNDATION   13

*Chapter 1*   The Cement of Love   14
*Chapter 2*   The Priesthood of all Believers   20
*Chapter 3*   The Wild Olive Tree   26
*Chapter 4*   The Body of Christ   31
*Chapter 5*   The Army of the Lord   37
*Chapter 6*   The Bride of Christ   42

**PART 2:** BUILDING ON THE FOUNDATION   47

*Chapter 7*   The Door of Worship   48
*Chapter 8*   Life in the Spirit   54
*Chapter 9*   A House of Prayer   59
*Chapter 10*   Discerning 'The Body'   64
*Chapter 11*   Meeting Together   69
*Chapter 12*   Washing One Another's Feet   74
*Chapter 13*   Sincere Love   79
*Chapter 14*   The Bond of Peace   84

**PART 3:** THE INTERNAL STRUCTURE AND THE ROOF   89

*Chapter 15*   The Structure of Leadership   90
*Chapter 16*   The Qualifications for Leadership   95
*Chapter 17*   Shepherding the Flock   100
*Chapter 18*   Working Together   105
*Chapter 19*   The Value of Vision   110
*Chapter 20*   The Importance of Discipleship   115

**PART 4:** WORKING THE FIELDS OUTSIDE   121

*Chapter 21*   Gathering the Harvest In   122
*Chapter 22*   Doing Good   127

# INTRODUCTION

The Bible opens with the story of a natural family, but closes with the story of God's family, the Church. All true believers are a part of the Church, whether they belong to a local expression of it or not. In this book, I describe God's family in a variety of ways in order to illustrate God's perspective on it – not only what the Church should look like, but also how we are to live as a community.

The sad thing is that, for one reason or another, all too many Christians today fail to recognise God's heart for His people, which means that they are then deprived of something of the blessing that God intended us to have. His family is the place where His love is meant to be expressed through the lives of His people as a witness to those who do not yet know Him.

We have all experienced family life in some way. For all too many of us, our experience was not very positive and as a result we can have a rather jaundiced view of what is entailed by living in the family of the Church. But understanding God's perspective can, if we are open to it, begin to bring us to a place of understanding and perhaps even of healing.

Since I believe that our lives as believers should be built upon the Bible, and in particular upon the foundation of the Kingdom principles that it contains, this book will be largely based upon what I understand to be God's vision for the Church, gleaned from the pages of Scripture. It is not meant to be an academic treatise, but rather a simple 'blueprint' to undergird the understanding of God's people about His design and purpose for us in terms of our life as a community.

Furthermore, whilst I will talk about many spiritual truths, they will not necessarily all be equally present in the life of any church, but all of them will need to be there in some measure to ensure that it is spiritually healthy. The balance will depend on God's vision for that church, along with its origins, history and leadership. Moreover, I have deliberately not fully developed the truths that I have written about, because I do not want this book to be used as a manual. I believe that every church should develop its own identity and character.

Perhaps here I should say that what I believe about the Bible can be summed up in these two brief passages of Scripture:

*'All Scripture is God-breathed and is useful for teaching, rebuking, correcting and training in righteousness, so that the man of God may be thoroughly equipped for every good work.'*

(2 Timothy 3:16–17)

*'The word of God is living and active. Sharper than any double-edged sword, it penetrates even to dividing soul and spirit, joints and marrow; it judges the thoughts and attitudes of the heart.'*

(Hebrews 4:12)

For that reason all the way through the book there will be a number of Biblical references that you can look up if you want to, along with several quotations, and although I have tried to keep these to a minimum, some chapters do have, of necessity, rather a lot – for which I make no apology. The quotations are taken from three translations – the New International Version (1984 edition), the New King James Version, and The Passion Translation – and have been carefully selected for the points that they speak of.

As you will soon discover, I have loosely used the picture of a house for the structure of this book. This is because in 1 Peter 2:4–6 we are described corporately as being built into a spiritual house. The book itself is divided into four parts:

1. The foundation of truth
2. Building on the foundation
3. The internal structure and the roof
4. Working the fields outside

The first part looks at the principles 'underneath' those discussed in the second, which is about the practicalities of community life; the third looks at leadership and vision, whilst the fourth is about our witness to those who have not yet found 'the Way' to the One who created them and who loves them unconditionally.

Jan Taylor
*May 2019*

# PART 1

# THE FOUNDATION OF TRUTH

# 1

# THE CEMENT OF LOVE

*For God so loved the world that he gave his one and only*
*Son, that whoever believes in him shall not perish but*
*have eternal life.*
(John 3:16)

God's heart towards us is one of love, as the above verse makes plain, and I believe that understanding what that means is foundational to understanding His perspective on the Church. So let me begin this book by talking, albeit briefly, about God's character and nature, before looking in more detail at what that love is like.

In recent years I have heard all too many Christians say that they think the God of the Old Testament is not the same as the God of the New, but I believe that those who say such things have failed to grasp not only the progressive revelation of God's character and nature given to us in the Bible, but also the spiritual, historical and social context of the two eras contained in its pages.

Whilst the primary attribute of the God whom we worship is love, He is also eternal, sovereign (the King of Kings), omnipotent (all-powerful), omniscient (all-knowing) and omnipresent (ever-present), as well as being a God of holiness, righteousness, truth and justice – all of which are undoubtedly tempered by His compassion, mercy and grace. However, I am not going to discuss these attributes in any depth as to do so would be beyond the scope of this book; I include them only to indicate what a balanced picture of God should look like.

Going back to the subject of love, there are four different kinds mentioned in the New Testament: *agape, storge, philos* and *eros*. These Greek words mean, respectively:

- unconditional love
- parental love
- brotherly love
- physical love.

The kind of love the Bible refers to when it is speaking about God is unconditional love, and the apostle Paul gives us a basic definition of it:

> *Love is patient, love is kind. It does not envy, it does not boast, it is not proud. It is not rude, it is not self-seeking, it is not easily angered, it keeps no record of wrongs. Love does not delight in evil but rejoices with the truth. It always protects, always trusts, always hopes, always perseveres. Love never fails.*
>
> (1 Corinthians 13:4–8a)

To that definition let me add that I have come to believe that this kind of love is full of compassion, grace and mercy. More than that, it sets people free to become all that God purposed that they should be in order for them to be able to fulfil their destiny and calling.

As well as having numerous attributes, God also has many names which describe something of His nature and character. Let me give you just a few of them to think about: Lord, Healer, Deliverer, Provider, Friend, as well as the one that I want to talk about now, which is Father, because that speaks of our adoption as 'sons' (Romans 8:13–16) and thus of us being part of His family. (Perhaps here I should say that when the Bible speaks about 'sonship' it is not speaking about gender, but about relationship and inheritance; a similar thing applies to the scriptures that refer to believers being 'brothers'.)

The father in the parable known as 'The lost son' (Luke 15:11–32) provides us with a model, not only of what a good father is like, but also of the quality of the love that God has for His children.

If you do not know this parable, it is the story of a young man who demands his inheritance from his father and, having obtained it, leaves home and squanders it. Having come to his senses, the young man returns home hoping for some kind of employment in the family business, but instead he gets a totally unexpected welcome from his father, who has been waiting for him to return. Not only does the father welcome the young man back with open arms, but he also throws a feast in celebration, much to the disgust of his older brother!

The father in the parable demonstrates unconditional love towards his once-rebellious child, and that is what God is like with every one of us. This of course is because we have given our lives to Jesus and put our trust in all that He did for us through His life, death and resurrection. From my perspective this is incredible considering that we, like the young man in the parable, have done nothing to deserve to be loved in this way, but it is important to remember that such a love can never be earned and is in fact entirely a product of grace.

Since God is our Father there should be some kind of family likeness. Love is a part of that, as the following verse makes abundantly clear:

> God is love. Whoever lives in love lives in God, and God in him.
>
> (1 John 4:16b)

In fact during His time here on earth Jesus was asked what the greatest commandment was, and this was His response:

> 'Love the Lord your God with all your heart and with all your soul and with all your mind.' This is the first and greatest commandment. And the second is like it: 'Love your neighbour as yourself.'
>
> (Matthew 22:37–39)

Jesus laid down His life for us of His own volition when He died on the cross (Romans 5:6–8) and gives us His life when we surrender ours to Him (Romans 6:23). The more deeply we have surrendered, which is a lifelong process, the more that life flows out through us and His love is incarnated in us. A commandment involves a decision, and whether we choose to obey or not is indicative of where we are in our relationship with God; the greater our willingness to do what is asked of us, the greater our degree of surrender to Him (1 John 5:3).

Before His arrest Jesus modelled how we were to lay down our lives for those who, like us, have given their life to Him. He did this by washing the feet of His disciples at what we call the 'last supper' (John 13:1–17), and at that time He issued the following commandment:

*A new command I give you: Love one another. As I have loved you, so you must love one another. By this all men will know you are my disciples, if you love one another.*

(John 13:34–35)

The New Testament speaks a lot about the ways in which we can show love to each other, but it also teaches about the practical outworking of our loving service to one another and within the Church. Whilst I will be talking in more detail about this later in the book, I do want to share a quote from the first letter of John as an indication of the kind of thing that I mean:

*If anyone has material possessions and sees his brother in need but has no pity on him, how can the love of God be in him?... let us not love with words or tongue but with actions and in truth.*

(1 John 3:17–18)

In other words, our love for each other is demonstrated by the way in which we behave towards each other and is a reflection of our love for God. The more we are willing to give of ourselves, our time and our resources to those around us, the more complete is the surrender of our lives to Him. Having said that, I think that we also all need to remember that everything we are and everything we have belongs to God; therefore we need to be responsible stewards of it by seeking God for His wisdom in how we live and with regard to all that we do. Jesus only did what He saw the Father doing, and that should be our goal too (John 5:19).

Our love, concern and care for one another should be very clear to see, so that anybody visiting the church that we belong to remembers it long after their visit. That kind of love will open people up to the gospel more than anything else that they may see or experience whilst they are with us, because love is what every one of us truly longs for above all else.

# 2

# THE PRIESTHOOD OF
# ALL BELIEVERS

*Coming to Him as to a living stone, rejected indeed by men,*
*but chosen by God and precious, you also, as living stones, are*
*being built up a spiritual house, a holy priesthood, to offer up*
*spiritual sacrifices acceptable to God through Jesus Christ.*
(1 Peter 2:4–5 NKJV)

One of the fundamental truths of the Kingdom that re-emerged as a result of the Reformation was that of the Priesthood of all believers, yet I have become aware over the past few years that in many church circles today it has been sidelined or even completely ignored, because all too many people fail to see its importance in terms of God's economy.

In order to understand that, we need to not only understand the role of a priest, but also to recognise that God's plan was always that every one of His people should function as a priest. This is indicated by the fact that in the book of Exodus, God speaks of His desire for Israel to be a kingdom of priests

(Exodus 19:4–6). As to why that did not happen at that time, that is spelt out further on in Exodus and you might like to read about it for yourself (see Exodus 20:18–20).

In the Old Testament Era the duties of the ordinary priest were very diverse and included such things as:

- collecting tithes
- setting the size of the sacrifices of individual worshippers
- presenting the offerings (Leviticus 21:5–6) on behalf of the people
- providing the music for worship
- blowing trumpets at the various feasts
- maintaining all that was within the boundaries of the Temple grounds
- evaluating problems with regard to any contact that people had had with the dead as well as their bodily emissions
- performing purification rites (Leviticus 14:1–7)
- dealing with disputes
- pronouncing blessings (Deuteronomy 21:5).

This list of duties clearly shows us that the role of a priest, often referred to as 'the ministry', has two dimensions: an upwards one towards God and a horizontal one towards His people – something which is just as true for us today as it was for the Israelites in the Old Testament Era.

For us as Christians, our ministry as priests is expressed rather differently. But, whilst most of the duties listed above are no longer part of the ministry of the Priesthood to which we are called, there are nevertheless still two dimensions to our role.

Let me look first at what I have called the 'horizontal' dimension, which is about our ministry to other believers. I am not going to go into much detail about this here, because I discuss it in a little more depth further on in the book. This aspect of our Priesthood has, as might be expected from the last chapter, love at its core, as well as being based on Kingdom principles, along with things such as our personality, character, abilities, gifts and calling. But the primary thing that is vital for us all to recognise is that every believer has a particular role or function that God wants them to fulfil within the life of the Church, or beyond, which will develop and/or change as they grow and mature in Him; there is no unemployment in the Kingdom of God, although some may need a period of 'sick leave' or even 'convalescence'!

The 'vertical' dimension also flows out of love and is a response to God's love for us (1 John 4:19). It is primarily about developing and building a relationship of intimacy with Him. There are of course many different aspects to doing so, but I particularly want to focus on the one that is the most neglected in our day, and that is what the Bible calls 'holiness'. I define this simply as being set apart by God, living in right relationship with Him and with those around us.

However, before I discuss the subject of holiness, I need to talk briefly about sin. The definition that I particularly like is that sin is a failure to 'hit the mark' (see Romans 3:23), or to put it another way, it is our inability to reach the standard of behaviour required of each one of us by God.

More than that, the Bible makes it plain that if God had not provided Jesus as a 'bridge' (as some preachers describe it) between us and Him (Hebrews 9:22, 27–28), there would be no salvation for any of us. This is because without holiness no one can enter into a relationship with God (Hebrews 12:14) or be with Him in the life that is to come at the end of our life here on earth (Acts 4:12).

In theological terms there are two sides to holiness: justification (sometimes called 'imputed righteousness') and sanctification, and these cannot be separated from each other. The first describes the way in which we are clothed with the righteousness of Christ from the moment we give our lives to Him, whilst the second describes how as we walk in partnership with the Holy Spirit we are progressively transformed from the inside out, becoming more like Christ (2 Corinthians 3:18) and thus living more holy lives.

Part of the process involved is being willing to recognise when we have fallen short of God's standard and to put things right with Him – to do what 1 John 1:9 speaks of and confess our sin to God. This will bring the cleansing that we need to be able to walk in right relationship with the Lord, as well as with each other.

Returning to the Scripture verses at the beginning of this chapter, I would like now to continue from where that quotation finished:

> *Therefore it is also contained in the Scripture,*
> *'Behold, I lay in Zion*
> *A chief cornerstone, elect, precious,*
> *And he who believes on Him will by no means be put to shame.'*
> (1 Peter 2:6 NKJV)

The word 'cornerstone' is not used very often today, but is of great significance in the above verse, so I think it will be helpful to define it to ensure that we all understand exactly what I am talking about. According to Wikipedia, a cornerstone is 'the first stone set in the construction of a masonry foundation, important since all other stones will be set in reference to this stone, thus determining the position of the whole structure'; synonyms given are: foundation, basis, keystone, mainspring, mainstay and linchpin.

Drawing on that definition, we can see that just as we are a spiritual house, Jesus is the line and the pattern for us all; He is the foundation on which our lives are to be built and the linchpin that holds it all together. Since Jesus is also described as 'the Word' (John 1:1-3, 14), it is essential for us as believers to have at least some personal knowledge of the Bible, so that we are able to build our lives on a foundation of the principles contained within its pages. This will help us to live in a way that progressively recognises Him not only as our Lord but also as the head of our house (Colossians 1:15-20).

Perhaps here I should say that once we have given our lives to Jesus, He sends the Holy Spirit to us to be our counsellor and guide (John 14:13-15, 26) because He knows that we cannot live a life of holiness without the help that only He can give.

Going back to the subject of the Priesthood of all believers: further on in the same book that I quoted from at the beginning of this chapter, the apostle Peter says that we are a 'royal priesthood' (1 Peter 2:9). This speaks to me of our authority in Christ, an area of teaching that I have not heard anyone speak on in years and yet it is something that we all need to have some understanding of in order to be able to walk in the victory of the cross.

For the purpose of this book, the point that needs to be made about the authority of a believer (Matthew 28:18–20) is that it will vary, depending not only on a person's maturity but also on their function within the Church. It is not a fixed thing, but develops as we grow; someone who has just come to Christ will not have the same degree of authority as someone who has walked closely with Him for a number of years.

# 3

# THE WILD OLIVE TREE

*If some of the branches have been broken off, and you, though
a wild olive shoot, have been grafted in among the others and
now share in the nourishing sap from the olive root, do not
boast over those branches. If you do, consider this: You do not
support the root, but the root supports you.*

(Romans 11:17–18)

For those of you who do not yet know the Bible very well,
the quotation above will probably seem rather a strange
one to use when speaking of the spiritual foundations
of church life, so let me start this chapter by explaining it in
simple terms: the 'olive root' referred to in these verses is Israel,
who are described throughout the Bible as being God's chosen
people, and the phrase 'wild olive shoot' refers to all those who
have given their lives to Christ.

Furthermore, throughout most of the Old Testament Era the
Hebrew people were the people God had chosen to represent
Him, so what this quotation is in fact saying is that the Church
is not His replacement for Israel, but is in fact in some way

an extension of that nation and His purposes in this world. The reason for this is given in Paul's letter to the Romans, earlier in the same chapter as the quotation about the Wild Olive:

*Rather, because of their transgression, salvation has come to the Gentiles to make Israel envious. But if their transgression means riches for the world, and their loss means riches for the Gentiles, how much greater will their fulness bring!*

(Romans 11:11b–12)

Some of you might be wondering about the relevance of all this to church life, but there are two main reasons why this is of importance to us in terms of building the foundation of our community.

The first reason is that we will never understand God's heart for us as a community if we do not understand something of the history of God's dealings with His people in the past, and the way in which all of that connects with His plan of salvation for humankind. For example: one of the things that the story of Esther teaches us is that fasting (and I assume also prayer) can change the history of a people, whilst the Song of Songs, which was written by King Solomon, reveals God's passion for His people both corporately and individually.

The second reason is that every book in the Bible, apart from the two that Luke wrote, were written by Jews and therefore we should not be prejudiced against the Jewish people, or for that matter any other ethnic group, since the word 'Gentile' includes all other people-groups.

In fact, prejudice of any kind breaks what is often referred to as the 'royal law', namely the commandment to love. Also, the apostle Paul says:

*There is neither Jew nor Gentile, slave nor free, male nor female, for you are all one in Christ Jesus.*

(Galatians 3.28)

To me what this verse says by implication is that all are welcome to join God's family regardless of ethnic background, class or gender. Sadly, this truth has not always been recognised in different parts of the world, including the UK, as well as at various times in history; in fact it is still sometimes an issue in certain places even today.

Going back to the subject of prejudice, I think it is important to explain that I am not saying we should tolerate ungodly behaviour in our midst. In Part 2 of this book I will talk briefly about the need for us to bring loving correction to individuals involved in those situations, and in Part 3 I will discuss the need, in extreme cases, for what I call 'church discipline' – for lack of a less emotive description.

Another thing that I need to clarify is to do with the whole issue of 'pruning'. The scripture shared at the beginning of the chapter holds the implication that God prunes Israel (grafting involves pruning as part of the process) and there are two things here that need to be understood. The first is that God is the one who is doing the pruning, and the second is that it is not just Israel that He prunes, nor for that matter is it just His people (John 15:1–8), although that is going to be the focus of the rest of this chapter. Over the years I have come to realise, as have many commentators, that God does his pruning through the circumstances of our lives. In the letter to the Hebrews we read:

*Endure hardship as discipline; God is training you as sons. For what son is not disciplined by his father? If you are not disciplined (and everyone undergoes discipline), then you are illegitimate children and not true sons.*

(Hebrews 12:7–8)

I remember that the first time I read these verses I was shocked at the idea of God disciplining me in this way, as it went against my rather immature understanding of His nature and character. But as I have grown in Him over the years, I have come to realise that He loves us so much that He uses our circumstances to enable us to mature. He knows that just as the butterfly has to struggle to break free of the chrysalis in order to be able to fly, we need to learn how to deal with the difficulties of life in order to be able to become the people He intended us to be, thus fulfilling our purpose and destiny.

However, there is another reason for God wanting us to work our way through whatever we end up having to face in life, and that is spelt out further on in the letter to the Hebrews:

*Our fathers disciplined us for a little while as they thought best; but God disciplines us for our good, that we may share in his holiness. No discipline seems pleasant at the time, but painful. Later on, however, it produces a harvest of righteousness and peace for those who have been trained by it.* (Hebrews 12:10–11)

From this passage we can see that another purpose of God's discipline is to enable us to become more like Him, to acquire through our circumstances a greater family likeness. Or, to put it another way, to incarnate His love and character progressively in our hearts and lives.

Having said all this, perhaps I should add that obviously there are times when God will deliver us from our circumstances, as those of you who know your Bible well will understand from various stories contained within its pages (for example, Daniel 6:1–23; Acts 16:25–34). But more often than not, He will not choose to do so. Should that be the case, it does not make someone a failure as a Christian.

Sadly, in Christian circles there are, and have been, teachings that suggest that if you are going through difficult circumstances then there is something wrong with the quality of your faith, or you have sinned in some way. Whilst there may be an element of truth in such teachings, they are based on a wrong understanding, not only of the nature and character of God but also of His Word.

When people are going through a difficult time they need our love and our support, not our judgement, or for that matter our condemnation (Matthew 7:1–5); the kind of teaching mentioned just above has a tendency to produce that kind of unloving attitude in people. I think we need to remember the saying: 'There, but for the grace of God, go I.'

# 4

# THE BODY OF CHRIST

*For as the body is one and has many members, but all the members of that one body, being many, are one body, so also is Christ. For by one Spirit we were all baptized into one body – whether Jews or Greeks, whether slaves or free – and have all been made to drink into one Spirit. For in fact the body is not one member but many.*

(1 Corinthians 12:12–14 NKJV)

The baptism that the apostle Paul is speaking of here happens at the moment of conversion, which is when we initially receive the Holy Spirit; it is the point at which we become part of the Body of Christ and are adopted into the family of God (Ephesians 1:4–5). Whilst what is generally referred to as the 'baptism of the Spirit' (see Acts 2:1–4) may happen at the same time, it will not necessarily do so, as that is about the overflow of the Spirit into our lives, whereas the baptism that we are talking about here is what I call His 'inflow' into our lives – I think that makes plain the difference between the two.

Before discussing what being part of the Body of Christ

means in practice, I want to share another quotation from 1 Corinthians, found further on in the same chapter as the quote above:

> *If the whole body were an eye, where would be the hearing? If the whole were hearing, where would be the smelling? But now God has set the members, each one of them, in the body just as He pleased.*
>
> (1 Corinthians 12:17–18 NKJV)

The picture of the body has a lot to teach us about God's plans and purposes, not only for us as individuals but also for us as a family. From the verses that I have shared already it is clear that God creates us for a particular role, that we need each other to be able to fulfil His purpose for us, and that each one of us is essential to the proper functioning of the Body.

Further on in 1 Corinthians chapter 12, we see that even more clearly (see verses 20–22) and then we read:

> *And those members of the body which we think to be less honourable, on these we bestow greater honour; and our unpresentable parts have greater modesty, but our presentable parts have no need. But God composed the body, having given greater honour to that part which lacks it, that there should be no schism in the body, but that the members should have the same care for one another.*
>
> (1 Corinthians 12:23–25 NKJV)

From these verses we can see that God's intention is that we should seek to shield each other's flaws and weaknesses from view, rather than exposing them, and that we are meant to care for each other in such a way that we are able to live in harmony with one another. Of course this only becomes possible if we see each other through the eyes of faith, as it is only then that the impossible becomes possible (Hebrews 11:6)!

No doubt this is why Paul in Romans 12:1–2 speaks of the need to renew our minds before being able to prove the will of God; there needs to be a paradigm shift, not only in how we see things but also in how we think, before we can live in the way that He wants us to. Obviously that is a progressive thing, so it seems to me that what God is looking for from us, primarily, is a *willingness* to do what He is asking us to do. He knows that the inner transformation that needs to take place in us, in our hearts, is going to take time, and He has the grace to recognise that we are all works in progress.

The head of the Body is of course Jesus (Colossians 1:18) and it is from Him that the government of the Church comes, albeit through human vessels that He has prepared for that role. I will say more about the authority of church leaders in later chapters; for now, I just want to point out that their role in our lives involves:

*the equipping of the saints for the work of ministry, for the edifying of the body of Christ, till we all come to the unity of the faith and of the knowledge of the Son of God ... to the measure of the stature of the fullness of Christ; that we should no longer be children, tossed to and fro and carried about with every wind of doctrine, by the trickery of men ... but, speaking the truth in love, may grow up in all things into Him who is the head – Christ ...*

(Ephesians 4:12–15 NKJV)

Those whom God puts in authority in the Church are called to disciple those put under their care; discipleship is not just about what is often called their 'platform ministry', but is also about modelling Christ to us in their own lives. Part of their role involves spending time ensuring that each person in their congregation not only grows in maturity but also finds their place in that body of believers. That means encouraging them to connect to God on a deeper level than they may already be doing and to discover His heart for them.

It may also mean enabling people to find ways to connect with other members of that congregation, as well as helping them to discover their abilities, their gifts, their ministry/ministries and their calling; then, as they grow and develop, to release them into the work that God wants them to do.

Let's go back to the issue of our function within the Body. As well as there being what is often called the 'fivefold' ministry' (some would say that it was 'fourfold', but that is not what I personally believe) – apostle, prophet, evangelist, pastor and teacher (Ephesians 4:11) – there are two lists of spiritual gifts, one in Romans 12:6–8 and the other in 1 Corinthians 12:8–10. It may be helpful for those of you who have not been Christians for long to know that in the past the list in Romans was often referred to as the 'motivational gifts', whilst the one in Corinthians was referred to as the 'gifts of the Spirit'. It is these spiritual gifts that I now want to speak about.

Before I do so, however, let me share with you what Paul says about the gifts of the Spirit, as some of my comments will be based on what he said:

*But the manifestation of the Spirit is given to each one for the profit of all.* (1 Corinthians 12:7 NKJV)

From this verse we can see not only that these gifts are supernatural, but also that they are given to each and every one of us for the benefit of all. Having said that, I am sure that some of you at least are wondering why you are not seeing them in operation, or if you are, why their use is so limited. I think there are a number of reasons for that being the case. For example:

- fear of the supernatural
- ignorance about the gifts and/or their purpose
- apathy or a lack of interest
- wanting to be seen as being 'relevant' to those who are not yet believers.

However, whatever the reason, the use of spiritual gifts is not meant to be seen as an optional extra for us as God's children, nor did He ever intend them to be used by a select few, as seems to be the thinking in some church circles. They are for every one of us to use in whatever way is appropriate for us as individuals as they form part of our calling.

To back up what I am saying, let me share some of Jesus' teaching to His disciples on this subject:

*He told them, 'This is what is written: The Christ will suffer and rise from the dead ... and repentance and forgiveness of sins will be preached in his name to all nations, beginning at Jerusalem. You are witnesses of these things. I am going to send you what my Father has promised; but stay in the city until you have been clothed with power from on high.'*

(Luke 24:46–49)

This passage shows us some important things to be aware of as disciples of Jesus. I want to briefly speak about two of them:

- The first is that every single one of us is called to be a witness – to speak to those around us not only about what Jesus has done for *us*, but also about His love for *them*.

- The second is that God will give us the power to do what He is asking us to do, and it is through that empowering that God equips us with spiritual gifts.

# 5

# THE ARMY OF THE LORD

*Endure hardship with us like a good soldier of Christ Jesus.*
*No-one serving as a soldier gets involved in civilian affairs – he*
*wants to please his commanding officer. Similarly, if anyone*
*competes as an athlete, he does not receive the victor's crown*
*unless he competes according to the rules.*

(2 Timothy 2:3–5)

In God's economy the discipline needed to shape and form us into His Army is done through our circumstances and the work of the Holy Spirit in our lives, hence what the above passage says about 'hardship'.

With regard to pleasing the 'commanding officer', the more our lives have been surrendered to God, the greater our passion for Him will be. Since pleasing Him will be the primary desire of our hearts, we will progressively lose the desire to live any other way.

Our level of obedience is an indication of our love for God. If we treat His commandments as if they are optional, or ignore the Lord's voice when He speaks to us on a personal level, then that is an indication of the quality of our relationship, as well as indicating our level of faith (Romans 1:5).

The scripture at the beginning of this chapter also speaks about competing 'according to the rules'. Whilst those outside the Church think they can live as they please, that is not true for us as believers; the purpose of our lives is to progressively become more like Jesus and to partner with Him in advancing His Kingdom.

Thus for us, our lives need to be built on a foundation of Kingdom truth, or to put it another way, on the truth of 'His Word'. This can be quite a challenge in the times we live in – and for all sorts of reasons.

The more we are doing that, the more our lives will look radically different from those who are not yet part of the family of God. How we live our lives, along with the value system that each of us bases our life upon, will set us apart from others, making each one of us a witness to the life-changing power of the gospel.

Before going any further, I want to say clearly that, although we are an 'Army', the war we are in is not a physical one, but a spiritual one; it is to do with the clash of two kingdoms, the Kingdom of Light and the kingdom of darkness (1 Peter 2:9–10). This is often referred to as the battle between good and evil.

Biblically there are three 'battle zones': (1) 'the world', which means any pattern of belief that denies the existence and/or power of God (1 John 2:15–17); (2) 'the flesh' (a term more frequently used in the past than nowadays), namely our struggle against sin (Hebrews 12:4); and (3) the forces of darkness

– often referred to as the 'enemy' of our soul (James 4:7; 1 Peter 5:8–9). However, the field of battle lies in our minds, as the following passage shows:

*For though we live in the world, we do not wage war as the world does. The weapons we fight with are not the weapons of the world. On the contrary, they have divine power to demolish strongholds. We demolish arguments and every pretension that sets itself up against the knowledge of God, and we take captive every thought to make it obedient to Christ.*

(2 Corinthians 10:3–5)

These verses make it plain that this battle is not one that we have to fight alone; we will have 'divine' help from the Holy Spirit (John 16:12–15) in it. So the process involves learning how to partner with Him in the situation that has been described.

However, it is important to note that if we are not progressively renewing our minds (Romans 12:1–2), we will find that our life is just one battle after another, and this will affect how we live our personal lives as well as our life within the community.

Renewing the mind is about identifying the lies of the enemy; it is about looking at what we believe and seeing where that does not marry up with Kingdom truth. Then we need to work it through with God, which involves repenting of the lie in question, forgiving whatever and whoever it came from, including ourselves, renouncing it, and then replacing it with truth.

Let me give you a simple example of this process from my own life: I grew up believing that I should have been a boy as neither of my parents wanted a girl. When I recognised that this was a lie, I released forgiveness to my parents for their attitude to me and then to myself for believing the lie.

After that, I renounced the lie and replaced it with something of the truth found in Psalm 139:13–16. As a result I have become more feminine and dress a little differently from how I once did. Not only that; I now relate differently to both men and women as a consequence of having dealt with this lie.

The weapons that God has given us are mainly defensive (see Ephesians 6:13–18), but we do have some that are not, such as praise (Acts 16:25–26), the Word of God, the 'blood' (the finished work of Jesus, i.e. all that He did through His life, death and resurrection) and our testimony (Revelation 12:11). These are our primary weapons for fighting the enemy.

Being part of the Army of the Lord is not like being part of a national army. It is not structured in the same way and there are no holidays, or even retirement, but just as on a human battlefield, people can get wounded, or even become exhausted by the length of time a 'battle' has taken or is taking. We need to recognise that at such times those people may need to spend time in the intensive care ward of our love and prayer.

In this situation there are so many practical things that we can do for people to show them that they are loved, but the key will be to ask ourselves what would help them the most at that moment. Obviously if we are pressed for time, we may not be able to do much, but sometimes what people most need is to know that people care. So, for example, a card or a brief phone call may make a world of difference to someone who is finding life tough.

Interestingly, the armour of the Lord as described in Ephesians is based on the armour of a Roman soldier, which had no back section to it. To me this speaks of the need to watch one another's backs – to pray for one another (Ephesians 6:18), rather than judging (Matthew 7:1–5) or even gossiping about each other (Proverbs 16:28). Such things are not only unloving but also deeply damaging, and not just for the people involved, as it can affect the whole church as well. These actions also do not reflect the truth that we are proclaiming about God's love to those who are not yet part of His family.

# 6

# THE BRIDE OF CHRIST

*'Let us be glad and rejoice and give Him glory, for the marriage*
*of the Lamb has come, and His wife has made herself ready.'*
*And to her it was granted to be arrayed in fine linen, clean and*
*bright, for the fine linen is the righteous acts of the saints.*
(Revelation 19:7–8 NKJV)

Reading these verses may leave some of you wondering what they are talking about, particularly if you are new to the faith, and so the first thing I want to say is that Jesus is coming back (1 Thessalonians 4:15–17) to take all those who believe, or have believed in Him prior to their death, to be with Him in heaven for all eternity. God's purpose for us ultimately is that we will be married to Christ, but quite what that means, or is going to look like, is not made clear anywhere in Scripture.

Obviously it will not be a sexual union, but will be a relationship that is based on a deep knowing of Him – and I presume each other, although the Bible is silent on this issue.

I think at this point I need to remind us all that just as it takes commitment to develop intimacy in any human relationship, it is the same in our life with God. We would spend time and effort on building a human relationship, and the same principle applies to our relationship with God. Developing a relationship with God means spending time with Him and learning about Him by reading His Word. Getting to know the Bible is a vital part of this process, as that is how we learn about Him – His character, His nature and His ways.

Moreover, God will use the Bible to speak to us about His love for us, issues that we need to work through with Him, and our future. Not only that; God will often give us specific promises from His Word for our lives, just as He did with the saints of old, and that is not only to help us to understand something of His purpose for our lives, but also to enable us to partner with Him in the process that will need to happen for the promise to be fulfilled. Each of the promises that He gives us is an invitation to a greater degree of intimacy with Him.

A marriage speaks to me of love and passion and it is apparent from the Song of Songs that God has a deep passion for us all, not just corporately (as the above scripture from the book of Revelation might lead you to think) but also as individuals.

Some of you may be uncomfortable with the idea of God feeling passion for us, but that is because we associate it with sex, rather than equating it with intimacy. What Jesus longs for is for each one of us to enjoy an intimate relationship with Him, so that we are able to experience something of the pleasures that come from such a relationship now, rather than having to wait until we go to be with Him (1 Thessalonians 4:15–17).

Unlike a human marriage where generally the bride is aware of the date and may even have set it herself, it is God who has set the time for our marriage to Him, and He will call us to

Himself when the time comes. However, I do think that perhaps we may experience a growing sense of expectation and maybe even a certain amount of excitement as the time draws near for the wedding to take place.

For a woman who is getting married there is generally a time of preparation leading up to the day of her wedding, which includes all sorts of things from choosing the food for the meal celebrating the event, to choosing the rings, to the selection of her dress, but for us as the Bride of Christ all we have to do is get ourselves ready by doing what God has called us to do – what John referred to as 'the righteous acts of the saints' in the quote at the beginning of this chapter.

In the letter of James we see more clearly what John meant when he spoke about 'righteous acts':

*What does it profit, my brethren, if someone says he has faith but does not have works? Can faith save him? If a brother or sister is naked and destitute of daily food, and one of you says to them, 'Depart in peace, be warmed and filled,' but you do not give them the things which are needed for the body, what does it profit? Thus also faith by itself, if it does not have works, is dead.*

(James 2:14–17 NKJV)

In this passage we can see a link between faith and works, but there is another key to understanding it, which can be found in Romans 1:17. There Paul talks about salvation by faith alone, as it is our faith that saves us, but our faith needs to be evidenced by the way in which we live our lives. More than that:

*Without faith it is impossible to please Him, for he who comes to*

*God must believe that He is, and that He is a rewarder of those who diligently seek Him.*

(Hebrews 11:6 NKJV)

The chapter that I have just quoted from teaches us a lot about the nature of faith. I wonder what your definition of faith is. I have realised over the course of my Christian life that faith is multifaceted – that, whilst it is about trust, about yielding my will to His, it is also so much more than that.

This is clearly evidenced in Hebrews 11 where we are told about a number of key Old Testament characters; their lives are described to us through their acts of faith, and therefore have a lot to teach us about it. We are also told that:

*faith is the substance of things hoped for, the evidence of things not seen. For by it the elders obtained a good testimony. By faith we understand that the worlds were framed by the word of God, so that the things which are seen were not made of things which are visible.*

(Hebrews 11:1–3 NKJV)

From the verses just quoted we can see that faith is not about what *we* are able to do, but about what *God* can do. I see it this way: we should believe that in Him all things are possible and that nothing that He has said He will do is impossible for him to do, even if our circumstances are telling us the complete opposite – something that was the case for quite a number of characters in the Bible!

Let me remind you of a few of these Biblical people in order to demonstrate the truth of what I am saying. There are, for example, a number of women I can think of immediately who were infertile until God intervened in their situations, enabling them to conceive, including Sarah (Genesis 18:1–15), Rachel (Genesis 29:31; 30:22–23) and Elizabeth (Luke 1:5–15, 36-37). Another example of great faith was, of course, Peter, who walked on the water (Matthew 14:28–31), albeit rather briefly!

True faith creates in us an expectation for something more – to live beyond what is the norm. It enables us to see things differently from those around us who do not have a relationship with God: it produces hope and gives us vision for the future. Moreover, just as God gives us vision for our lives as individuals, He does the same for us on a corporate level too; God has a plan for each church and will reveal that vision to us progressively. But I will say more about that in a later chapter.

In Part 2, 'Building on the foundation', we will look at some of the more practical aspects of church life, starting with worship and prayer, which are at the heart of community life.

# PART 2

# BUILDING ON THE FOUNDATION

# 7

# THE DOOR OF WORSHIP

*Six days before the Passover, Jesus arrived at Bethany, where*
*Lazarus lived, whom Jesus had raised from the dead. Here*
*a dinner was given in Jesus' honour. Martha served, while*
*Lazarus was among those reclining at the table with him. Then*
*Mary took about a pint of pure nard, an expensive perfume;*
*she poured it on Jesus' feet and wiped his feet with her hair.*
*And the house was filled with the fragrance of the perfume.*
(John 12:1–3)

The woman in this story pours out to Jesus all that she
has. That is what worship is about. The Greek word
*proskuno*, translated in the New Testament as 'worship',
literally means 'to kneel at the feet', and that is exactly what
Mary of Bethany did. As we can see in the setting of the story,
worship is not just something that we do in our corporate life,
or in our personal times with God, but is meant to be a way
of life; this story is set in the context of a social event, a meal,
and therefore speaks of our normal everyday life.

Since worship is a lifestyle, it should be at the heart of
everything we say and everything we do; our love for God should

be evident in every aspect of our lives. This will then set us apart from those around us who are not part of the family of God, enabling us to be a witness to them of the way in which God has changed our lives.

Obviously this is a journey, and is one that we will progressively make, as we intentionally partner with the Holy Spirit in the process involved in the transformation of our lives (2 Corinthians 3:18).

Living as I have just described has never been without its challenges, but in the world today they are far greater than they ever have been, because of the way in which society has changed. Whereas once upon a time many of 'God's laws' (as they were often called) were enshrined in the laws of our nation, that is no longer the case. What is more, you can now virtually live in whatever way you want, because truth is whatever you want it to be.

Not only that; we are now expected to accept, without question, the lifestyles of people whose behaviour would have been considered socially unacceptable twenty or so years ago, even though such behaviour goes against the teaching of the Bible. Recent ideas of 'toleration' now mean that we cannot say anything that might show we are not in agreement with the way someone is living.

This of course means that individual believers, and even churches, can be faced with situations where speaking out about certain issues in the wrong way can result in some kind of legal action and perhaps even prison. Sadly, therefore, some people do not want to focus in any way on those around them, so they themselves end up compromising their lives to some degree in order to keep a low profile. But doing so will ultimately cost them dear as it will eventually result in a loss of their faith in God; their hearts will become harder and harder, the longer they continue down this path.

As believers, part of our calling is to walk in the light (1 John 1:5–7), to be true to who and what we are, not just inside the community of faith but also outside it. Jesus gave us some important advice about doing so:

*I am sending you out like sheep among wolves. Therefore be as shrewd as snakes and as innocent as doves.*

(Matthew 10:16)

From my perspective, in order to be able to live in a way that reflects our love for God (Ephesians 5:15–17) we need His wisdom, and that is something that I pray for frequently. However, if we want to live in that way we will also need to have a clear understanding of the Kingdom principles that God has given to us in His Word; otherwise we will not have the foundation of truth that we need to build our lives on.

Not only that, but as I shared in the introduction:

*The word of God is living and active. Sharper than any double-edged sword, it penetrates even to dividing soul and spirit, joints and marrow; it judges the thoughts and attitudes of the heart. Nothing in all creation is hidden from God's sight. Everything is uncovered and laid bare before the eyes of him to whom we must give account.*

(Hebrews 4:12–13)

From this scripture it is obvious that there is a power in God's Word and that nothing is hidden from Him, but it is so much more than that. Whilst it is beyond the scope of this book to look at the Word in depth, I would like to point out to those of you who are as yet unaware of its life-changing power just how powerful it is. I also want to share another verse that points to something of its value for us; it comes from what is undoubtedly the longest of the Psalms:

> *Your word is a lamp to my feet*
> *and a light for my path.*

> (Psalm 119:105)

One of the many ways that God uses to speak to us personally is through His Word, and that is another good reason for us to spend time reading it. Perhaps I need to say here that no matter how good the teaching is on a Sunday morning, it will never provide enough of a foundation on which to build our lives; therefore it is essential for us all to do a certain amount of reading, not just of the Bible itself but also of some Christian literature, although of course the former (2 Timothy 2:15) is far more important than the latter.

Over the years, I have found that using a 'Read-the-Bible-in-a-year' plan enables me to be quite disciplined with regard to my Bible reading, but there are a number of different aids that one can use. If you do not have one, talk to your church leaders as they should be able to recommend some to you. (Also, if you do not already have them, a Bible dictionary and a basic commentary can be very helpful in helping you to find answers to some of the questions that will arise in your reading.)

Alongside reading the Bible it can also be helpful to do a certain amount of Bible study, which can be on a particular book of the Bible (for example, 1 John) or on a theme, such as prayer or healing. You can do this either at home or by going to a study group, if your church has them.

It can also be helpful to read books about the Christian life written by respected Christian leaders, such as R. T. Kendall, Philip Yancey or Mark Stibbe, as well as books in which people share something of their journey with God. However, these cannot replace reading the Bible for ourselves as it is only then that we begin to grasp the truths on which we can build our lives – the values that we will live by.

We read in 1 John:

> *Do not love the world or anything in the world. If anyone loves the world, the love of the Father is not in him. For everything in the world – the cravings of sinful man, the lust of his eyes and the boasting of what he has and does – comes not from the Father but from the world. The world and its desires pass away, but the man who does the will of God lives for ever.*
>
> (1 John 2:15–17)

Sadly, we live in a world where people want to be able to live their lives based on their own truth rather than God's; they want to set the standards for their lives based on how they want to live, and this is happening inside the Church as well as outside. But the true believer will always come to a place where he or she wants to live life in such a way that it pleases God, as can be seen from the scripture that I have just shared as well as from numerous others.

Perhaps here I should mention, for those of you who are not yet aware of it, that water baptism represents the death of your old life and the beginning of a new one. Romans 6:1–14 makes this plain; some people in fact see baptism as being your funeral. If you have died in the way described, then you will not want to continue to live the kind of life that you lived before, but will long for the one that God wants to give you (Jeremiah 29:11). However, this is not a one-off transaction, but a lifelong process, so we do need to be patient with ourselves and with those around us who are also part of the family of God.

# 8

# LIFE IN THE SPIRIT

*But the fruit of the Spirit is love, joy, peace, longsuffering, kindness, goodness, faithfulness, gentleness, self-control. Against such there is no law. And those who are Christ's have crucified the flesh with its passions and desires. If we live in the Spirit, let us also walk in the Spirit.*

(Galatians 5:22–25 NKJV)

It is as we die to self (Mark 8:34–37) that we begin to live in the Spirit, and the fruit of that process is what is described in the list given in the above scripture. It is not a painless process, as it involves progressively surrendering our lives to God, but producing the fruit described is worth whatever it costs, because the rewards, which are both temporal and eternal, are beyond whatever price we will ultimately pay.

In the first part of this book I spoke about the need to confess any sin that we commit to God (1 John 1:9) and about the necessity for us to renew our minds. Both of these things are part of the process that I am talking about, but neither of them is a one-off transaction. This is because, as one wit put it: 'The trouble with living sacrifices is that they crawl off the altar.' It is that tendency in us that means we will need to go on doing these things.

However, there are other aspects of the process that I now need to mention, albeit briefly, for the sake of completeness. These are repentance, forgiveness, healing and deliverance. We will need to partner with the Holy Spirit with regard to these things, just as we need to when we confess our sins or renew our minds.

As we yield to the Holy Spirit, His fruit is produced in us (Galatians 5:22–24) and we become more like Christ (2 Corinthians 3:18), which is the main aim of the Christian life. It is this that will draw people through us to Him.

Becoming like Christ is not only about incarnating Him in our lives in the way just described, but is also about doing the things that He did. In fact Jesus said to those who were following Him:

*Anyone who has faith in me will do what I have been doing. He will do even greater things than these, because I am going to the Father. And I will do whatever you ask in my name, so that the Son may bring glory to the Father.*

(John 14:12–13)

This is of course the purpose of what is generally called the 'baptism of the Spirit' (see Acts 2:1–4), which Jesus spoke of as being an empowering (Acts 1:8) to enable His disciples to witness for Him. Reading passages such as Matthew 28:18–20 helps us to see what that entails for us today.

God has plans for each one of us (Jeremiah 29:11). The gifts that are given through, or as a consequence of, the baptism of the Spirit are to equip us not just to witness but also to fulfil His call upon our lives. As Paul put it:

*We are God's workmanship, created in Christ Jesus to do good works, which God prepared in advance for us to do.*

(Ephesians 2:10)

Life in the Spirit is meant to be an adventure, a voyage of discovery, as we learn how to partner with the Holy Spirit to find out who we are in Christ and what we were made to do; this journey into God's heart for us will last for the rest of our earthly life and enable us to grow in intimacy with Him. Part of discovering who we are and what we are made to do is not just about our spiritual gifts, but will also involve things like our personality, character, history and the abilities that we were born with.

More than that, it will mean seeking God to see how He wants us to get involved in different aspects of church life, and listening to what He is saying to us about other aspects of our life, not just in our devotional times but also through what is spoken over us prophetically, either in our corporate meetings or on a personal level.

Furthermore, it could mean making sacrifices – giving up a job and/or a home that we love in order to be able to do what we know He is asking us to do. It may even mean moving to another country, adapting to a different culture and learning a new language, but whatever it means, it will lead you to a depth and quality of relationship with God that you would not otherwise find. To illustrate this point, let me share part of a letter that Paul wrote from prison towards the end of his life:

*Whatever was to my profit I now consider loss for the sake of Christ. What is more, I consider everything a loss compared to the surpassing greatness of knowing Christ Jesus my Lord, for whose sake I have lost all things. I consider them rubbish, that I may gain Christ and be found in him, not having a righteousness of my own that comes from the law, but that which is through faith in Christ – the righteousness that comes from God and is by faith.*

(Philippians 3:7–9)

From these verses we can see that Paul models for us the truth and reality of what I have just been talking about, but understanding how he did so will take a bit of unpacking.

Let me begin by briefly speaking about his life. Paul had an amazing conversion experience (Acts 9:1–19) and right from the beginning of his Christian life sought to do what God wanted him to, which meant that sometimes he ended up being in circumstances that had unpleasant consequences for him (2 Corinthians 11:16–33).

Since Paul had not only persecuted Christians before his conversion, but also had them killed (Acts 6:8–15; 7:54 – 8:1a), he experienced a lot of suspicion and rejection when he initially sought to become part of the community of believers in his area (Acts 9:19b–30), and yet years later he became an international leader who had worked with a number of key figures in the various places where he was led to go to plant churches.

As I look at Paul's life I see a number of keys with regard to living the Christian life, but for us in terms of learning how to walk in the Spirit there are two that stand out a mile; they are his obedience (Acts 16:8–10) and the way in which he partnered with other believers (Philippians 4:2–3) – something that all of us will need to do in order to be able to fulfil God's purpose for our lives.

Working with other believers is not always easy, but God often uses other people to enable us to grow, or to change in a multitude of different ways. That can include conflict (Proverbs 27:17), which is a truth that is not usually recognised. Many people fear conflict and will walk away from something that God has called them to do, rather than looking for a way to resolve the issues involved, which is a far more Biblical approach to things (Ephesians 4:3). I will say more about this in a later chapter.

# 9

# A HOUSE OF PRAYER

*Jesus entered the temple area and drove out all who were
buying and selling there. He overturned the tables of the
money-changers and the benches of those selling doves. 'It is
written,' he said to them, '"My house will be called a house of
prayer," but you are making it a "den of robbers".'*
(Matthew 21:12–13)

Just as conversation is a vital building block for developing
relationships with those around us, so the same is true
with regard to prayer and our relationship with God. The
Bible has much to teach us about prayer, particularly of course
in the Gospels where we not only learn about Jesus' relationship with our Father, but can also benefit from His teaching
on the subject. Beyond that of course there is a multitude of
books on the subject, but the best way to learn about prayer
is to do it – to ask God to teach us Himself as we spend time
with Him.

I have been a Christian for over thirty years now and, whilst
I have learnt a lot about prayer, I know that there is still a lot

more to learn – I understand that prayer is a journey. As such, it can be very exciting, particularly when you pray for something to happen and it actually does!

As a young Christian I really struggled with regard to my prayer life. I did not find it easy, but I persisted nevertheless, and as I did so, I began to see some amazing answers to my prayers: people I had been praying for were saved and healed. As a result, not only did my attitude to prayer change, but also the way in which I prayed for things.

One of the things that I have realised over the years is that God is not a chocolate vending machine; the purpose of prayer is not primarily about what God can do for us, but about developing an intimate relationship with Him. So part of the time that we spend with Him needs to be about listening to what He wants to say to us, something that I still find difficult at times even now.

It is important for us all to recognise that not only are there many different types of prayer, some of which I will talk about briefly in a moment, but there are also a number of ways of doing it – different styles. As long as whatever we do is firmly rooted in Biblical principles, there is nothing wrong with either using different kinds of prayer, or being creative in the way in which we pray.

In the first part of this book I mentioned the need for us to confess our sins to God (1 John 1:7–10), which obviously needs to be a regular part of our prayer life. But there is another kind of confession that is important too in terms of our devotional life, which is often referred to as a 'testimony' (Revelation 12:11). This can also be seen as a form of thanksgiving, although testimonies are usually given publicly, whereas giving thanks can be done in our personal times with God as well as in our corporate times of prayer.

Another vital aspect of our prayer life is praise, which is about celebrating not only who God is but also what He has done. Certain psalms have much to teach us about praising God. A good example to look at is Psalm 92; here are a few verses from The Passion Translation to illustrate my point:

> *It's so enjoyable to come before you*
> *with uncontainable praises spilling from our hearts!*
> *How we love to sing our praises over and over to you,*
> *to the matchless God, high and exalted over all!*
> *At each and every sunrise we will be thanking you*
> *for your kindness and your love.*
> *As the sun sets and all through the night,*
> *we will keep proclaiming, 'You are so faithful!'*
>
> (Psalm 92:1–2 TPT)

Incidentally, praise can be extremely powerful and can break the chains in people's lives, both literally (Acts 16:22–35) and metaphorically. So if we are seeking a breakthrough in some area of our lives, or with regard to a situation that we are praying into for others, this may well be the means of receiving it.

Petitionary prayer is making requests for God to intervene in some way in a particular situation in our life or in the lives of others (Philippians 4:6). Petitions can be made both in our personal prayer times as well as in our corporate gatherings. However, it is vital for us all to recognise that prayers of petition are not the same thing as intercession, which is about 'standing in the gap'. The best Biblical example of this is found in Genesis

18:20–32, which is the story of how Abraham intercedes for the city of Sodom; God tells him that He is about to destroy the city, but Abraham prays that He will spare it because that is where his nephew Lot is living with his family.

In my experience, intercession will always flow out of what God is saying to us, on a personal level or through the prophetic gift on a corporate level, although it may start with what seems to be a prayer of petition. I find this kind of prayer far more exciting than petitionary prayer, which for me can be a bit of a struggle, but you may find that your experience is the polar opposite; we are all made differently and that is something that needs to be recognised in our corporate life.

Sometimes the Holy Spirit can inspire us to use the Word of God in our intercession as that can not only provide a structure for our prayers but also guide us through to a point of breakthrough in our intercession.

Whilst I am not going to talk about what is often referred to as 'spiritual warfare' or 'identificational repentance', since they both require a lot of explanation, I am mentioning them as they are also vital forms of prayer, particularly for corporate meetings. If you do not yet know about them I recommend that you read some books on the subject, because if used well they can be vehicles of transformation for the lives of individuals as well as for cities and nations.

Of course the most important aspect of our prayer lives is learning how to discern the voice of God. This does not happen overnight, as those of you who have been Christians a while will know; like so much of the Christian life, it is a journey which will only truly be completed when we finally meet Jesus face to face in glory. Let me finish this very brief look at some of the different types of prayer by saying that creativity is of vital importance in developing our prayer lives, because if things become too rigid and inflexible, praying becomes a duty rather than leading us into greater intimacy with God.

Being creative can be as simple as doing things like drawing or painting pictures, lighting candles and writing down our prayers. We can also use different postures: standing, sitting, kneeling or lying prostrate before God, as seems to be appropriate for the moment.

Going back to the verses given at the beginning of this chapter, they speak of a 'house', and we are that house (1 Peter 2:4–5). Whilst in Jesus' day the place of worship was a physical place, that is no longer the case. In other words the Church is not a building, but a people (1 Peter 2:9–10), and those outside our community should know us to be a people of prayer.

Perhaps here I should say that I see the corporate prayer-meeting as the 'engine room' of the local church and the focal point of community life. Also, I think that it is a place where new believers can learn about prayer from those who are more mature in the faith and that, as such, it needs to be a place where people can 'get things wrong' or make mistakes without being made to feel small or inadequate.

Sadly, in all too many churches today corporate prayer is no longer seen as the priority that it should be, and as a result there is often no longer a meeting designated for it. For me this raises all sorts of questions about the priorities of the leadership of those churches and their understanding of the power of prayer, but it is not my place to judge them.

# 10

# DISCERNING 'THE BODY'

*Whoever eats this bread or drinks this cup of the Lord in an
unworthy manner will be guilty of the body and blood of the
Lord. But let a man examine himself, and so let him eat of the
bread and drink of the cup. For he who eats and drinks in an
unworthy manner eats and drinks judgment to himself, not
discerning the Lord's body.*
(1 Corinthians 11:27–29 NKJV)

Whilst the passage quoted above is about communion, there is a rather important spiritual principle contained within it that has much wider implications for us, and it is to do with discerning 'the Body'. This is not just a reference to Christ's physical body, but also includes all those who have accepted Him as their Lord and Saviour, both during and since His time here on earth, as is shown clearly if we study the context of this passage.

In other words, what Paul means when he speaks about discerning 'the Body' is the need to recognise that that includes not just Christ Himself, but also all His 'brothers'. Verse 29 is telling us that if we fail to do so, we are not right with God so should not be taking communion until we put things right with Him.

However, before I discuss communion any further I think it is necessary to look at the wider implications of what it means to recognise 'the Body' by talking about what I call 'denominational prejudice'. Whilst this seems to be less of an issue than it once was, it is still an ongoing problem in some parts of the Church.

Perhaps here I should say that there are certain groups that call themselves Christian but clearly are not, as their beliefs and/or practices are in some way in conflict with what the Bible teaches. For example, any group that denies that Jesus was and is both Man and God cannot be considered Christian as this is a key doctrine of our faith (John 1:14); the same applies to those who see the Holy Spirit as a force rather than as a person (Acts 5:3–4).

At the same time, we need to be careful not to judge people because of what they are currently involved in. I have known people who, when they first became Christians, were in such a group and it took them a while to make the break and to join a local church.

Another kind of prejudice that can be a problem is of a more personal nature and is based on a value judgement: someone may hold the view that because a particular person does 'such-and-such', he or she cannot be a Christian. But such an attitude is wrong (Matthew 7:1–2). The person in question may have not yet reached the point of recognising that what they are doing is wrong, or they may just have had a lapse of judgement.

All of us need to recognise that none of us are perfect as yet. We are called to extend the same grace that God has given us towards others, rather than judging people's standing with God, or for that matter judging in any other way (Luke 6:37).

Looking at the context of the passage that we are discussing adds another dimension to discerning 'the Body', because in previous chapters Paul spoke of things that were issues in the church in Corinth: division (1 Corinthians 3:1–4), sexual immorality (1 Corinthians 5:1–12; 6:12–20) and greed (1 Corinthians 11:20–21) being just some of them.

The bottom line from my perspective is that we need to ask God to look at our hearts before we take communion and to show us where we have fallen short of His standards, so that we can participate with a heart that is in right relationship with Him.

Returning to the passage quoted at the beginning of the chapter and to the subject of communion, there are a number of different ways of seeing communion, ranging from the view that it is just a memorial meal to the view that is generally held by those who call themselves Catholics, which is known as transubstantiation, the belief that the 'elements' (the bread and wine) are transformed into the literal body and blood of Christ.

However, whatever perspective we hold needs to be firmly rooted in Biblical principles, and I must admit that I struggle to see a Biblical basis for some of the views that people have when it comes to communion.

Personally, I do not see either of the two views mentioned as being particularly scriptural; I believe that the Bible tells us that communion is more than a memorial meal, and I cannot see any real basis for the doctrine of transubstantiation. Nevertheless, at the same time I do not think that it is ever right to reject people on the basis of their belief on this issue.

One of the reasons that I believe communion is more than a

memorial meal is found in the two verses that follow on from the quotation at the beginning of this chapter. Here Paul says:

> *That is why many among you are weak and sick, and a number of you have fallen asleep. But if we judged ourselves, we would not come under judgment.*

> (1 Corinthians 11:30–31)

These verses tell us that there is a power in communion and that taking it without proper regard either for Christ Himself, or for one another, may have serious consequences for us. From my perspective this means there is a 'mystical' dimension to taking it. In fact I have occasionally heard testimonies of people who have been healed whilst taking communion.

Another point worth making, particularly for those of you who are not aware of it, is that communion originated from the Passover meal that Jesus took with His disciples before His arrest and crucifixion (Luke 22:7–20), and that in order to fully grasp the significance and meaning of it we would need to look into what that was all about (Exodus 12:1–42). But for the purpose of this book we will look at just a few verses of the passage in question so that we can begin to see something of its meaning for us:

> *On the tenth day of this month every man shall take for himself a lamb, according to the house of his father, a lamb for a household ... And they shall take some of the blood and put it on the two door-posts and on the lintel of the houses where they eat it.*

> (Exodus 12:3, 7 NKJV)

In John 1:29 we are told that Jesus is 'the Lamb of God, who takes away the sin of the world'. This shows us that Jesus was the 'Passover Lamb', so the meal that Jesus celebrated with His disciples was for us a picture of His death; the application of blood to the doorposts and lintel speaks of the cross and the need to apply His blood to our lives.

Not only that; looking in depth at the story shows us that the Feast of Passover is about being delivered from bondage and entering into a new life, which is a description of the Christian life.

Another important aspect of the Passover story is that it was celebrated in families, speaking again of God's heart for family, and we see this is also true of communion, except that instead of being focused on the natural family the emphasis changes to the family of God.

From what I have said about it I hope you can see that communion is full of meaning, that it is a form of worship and something we are meant to celebrate together as a community.

# 11

# MEETING TOGETHER

*Let us not give up meeting together, as some are in the habit of doing, but let us encourage one another – and all the more as you see the Day approaching.*
(Hebrews 10:25)

The verse quoted above encourages us not to stop meeting with other believers, and I think that the two main reasons for this are that we need each other, not only in order to become the people that God intended us to be (Ephesians 4:11–16), but also in order to fulfil His purpose and destiny (Ephesians 2:10) for our lives.

Let me start by looking particularly at what I call our 'main meeting', which in most churches is generally held on a Sunday morning, but for various reasons may be held on another day or even at another time. It usually starts with what we often call 'the worship', although strictly speaking the whole thing is about worship in one way or another.

The main purpose of any of our meetings should be to encounter God, and this is particularly true of the part that we refer to as 'the worship'. But when you try to describe the process that takes place during it, you realise that the term 'worship' is not actually very helpful. The reasons for this will become clear in a moment, but for now we should realise that what is happening in that part of the service is not just preparation for the message, or for that matter whatever else is going to happen in that meeting.

Most meetings usually start with lively songs, which tend to have a strong element of praise in them. The quieter songs, which have been referred to in the past, in some quarters at least, as 'worship', would probably be better referred to as 'adoration' in order to clarify what exactly we are talking about.

If any of the people in the meeting have not spent time before the meeting preparing their hearts, then that will happen during what I call the 'praise' part of the meeting. A good worship leader will know when the congregation is ready to move into the next phase of the meeting as he/she will sense it in their spirit; this is the moment when we are ready to enter God's presence and we can recognise it as individuals as the moment when we reach the point of inner stillness.

It is at this point that people will find it easiest to hear God and to operate in spiritual gifts. Since some people will already be at this point because they have spent time with the Lord before coming to the meeting, when the meeting begins the Holy Spirit may already have begun to invade the atmosphere with His presence, and spiritual gifts may already have been in operation. However, it is important to recognise that just because we have seen these things does not necessarily mean that the congregation is ready to move into the next phase of the meeting.

An experienced worship leader will know not only where

the congregation is in this process, but also other things like which songs to sing and how many times to sing them; he/she will know how to follow the leading of the Spirit and will lead in partnership with Him even to the point of changing the agenda and the song list if necessary.

Having spoken, albeit briefly, of the spiritual dynamics of this part of our meeting, I want to now look at the physical side of things – what I call 'aids to worship'. Let's start with bodily posture. Whilst some people may want to stand all the way through this part of the meeting, some may want to sit, kneel or lie prostrate before the Lord, and it is not wrong for people to worship in different ways as God has made us all differently.

It is also not wrong to clap, dance or even wave banners, but some people are not comfortable with anyone worshipping God in a different way from themselves in a corporate setting. For some of these people these things may not have been part of their culture. Others may think that unity is based on uniformity and conformity, because they do not realise that things in God's Kingdom often operate in completely the opposite way to things outside it (Isaiah 55:8–9; 1 Corinthians 1:27–29), that in His Kingdom unity is based on creativity and diversity. I will say more about this later on in the book.

It is vital for us all to understand that we need to watch our attitude towards the way in which other people choose to worship as there may be consequences for us if our hearts are wrong (Luke 6:37–42). Certainly there seems to be an implication of this in 2 Samuel 6:16–23, which is the story of David dancing in what was basically his underwear before the Lord in a public place. Afterwards one of his wives, Michal, is critical of him for doing so, and we are told that she 'had no children to the day of her death' (v. 23), which strongly suggests a link between her attitude to David dancing and her infertility.

Generally, in the kind of meetings that I have been talking about, after the 'worship' a message is preached, either by someone in the church or by a guest speaker, but there may also be communion and/or a baptism, as well as perhaps a time of what is often referred to as 'ministry'. The important thing is that when we are not actively participating in the meeting, we are still engaging with whatever is happening, because we can encounter God in different ways at different points in the meeting.

It is worth noting here that we can also encounter God in our social times before and after the meeting, as people can say something which can land in our spirits in such a way that we know that God has not only spoken to us, but has also done something in our hearts. So these times are also vital to our journey into God's heart for us.

Whilst in bigger churches it may not be possible to give much time for the public use of spiritual gifts, I am of the opinion that the leader needs to make time if someone brings something to them from God that fits with what has been happening in the meeting, or with the message if it has not yet been preached, as that demonstrates to those who do not yet know Christ that He is a present reality, not just a historical figure. More than that, it encourages believers to a greater level of faith.

The format for our small groups and our prayer meetings will not generally contain all the ingredients of our main meeting, but they should be viewed as being vital not only for our spiritual development but also for the building of community life.

These smaller meetings can also provide opportunities for us to learn how to pray, as well as using spiritual gifts. Doing things for the first time is a lot less daunting in a smaller group, and there is generally a lot more freedom for people to make mistakes, get things wrong, without being embarrassed or publicly humiliated. It is therefore important for there to be a very loving and accepting culture in such meetings, so that people feel able to try things without worrying that getting things wrong could be very costly.

Smaller meetings can also be a good place to develop relationships with people, as well as to perhaps serve in the community in some way, for example by hosting such groups, or leading worship in them.

# 12

# WASHING ONE ANOTHER'S FEET

*When He had washed their feet, taken His garments, and sat down again, He said to them, 'Do you know what I have done to you? You call Me Teacher and Lord, and you say well, for so I am. If I then, your Lord and Teacher, have washed your feet, you also ought to wash one another's feet.'*

(John 13:12–14 NKJV)

Whenever I read about this particular episode of Jesus' life I feel such a sense of awe at His willingness to do something such as is described. After all, He is our creator and yet He was willing to humble Himself to what was considered the level of the lowliest servant and wash His disciples' feet, which would probably have been covered in filth.

Moreover, when Jesus then goes on to ask His disciples, and thus each one of us, to do the same, I feel that what He asks is the only response that we can make to His willingness to humble Himself in such a way, because doing so will demonstrate our love for Him. To me this is a picture of the sacrificial way in which Jesus wants us to serve one another. It is reinforced by what Paul says in Philippians:

> *Let this mind be in you which was also in Christ Jesus, who, being in the form of God, did not consider it robbery to be equal with God, but made Himself of no reputation, taking the form of a bondservant, and coming in the likeness of men.*
>
> (Philippians 2:5–7 NKJV)

In other words, unlike the Gentile leaders of Jesus' day, who would have undoubtedly thought washing someone's feet was below them, we are called to be the kind of people who are willing to do whatever is necessary in order to fulfil the Lord's purposes and to advance the Kingdom here on earth, whether that involves washing the toilet floor somewhere, or standing on a platform preaching whatever God lays on our heart.

Having what I call a 'servant heart' will of course also lead to us progressively recognising that no one is better than anyone else, whether they come from the landed gentry or the gutter, whether they are educated or not, and so on. Thus we will create a culture where people's worth in the community has nothing to do with *who* they are and everything to do with *whose* they are.

James has quite a lot to say about this, but I am going to share just a couple of verses to enable you to see that what I have said is what the Bible teaches:

> *If there should come into your assembly a man with gold rings, in fine apparel, and there should also come in a poor man in filthy clothes, and you pay attention to the one wearing the fine clothes,*

*and say to him, 'You sit here in a good place,' and say to the poor man, 'You stand there,' or, 'Sit here at my footstool,' have you not shown partiality among yourselves, and become judges with evil thoughts?*

(James 2:2–4 NKJV)

Such verses are incredibly challenging, particularly when you start thinking about the application of the principle enshrined in them! I do not think that many of us, in fact perhaps *any* of us, are without some kind, or level, of prejudice, either towards a particular group of people or towards particular individuals. But if we are to love others in the way that God calls us to, we need to be honest with Him about where we are with this issue, and ask Him to enable us to change our attitude.

Perhaps here I should say that people with a servant heart will be willing to use their resources for the Kingdom, whether that is time, abilities, money, their home, or their car, because there will be a recognition that everything we are, as well as all that we have, came from God and as such belongs to Him; that we are the stewards of it all and that He has entrusted it to us, to use it to advance His Kingdom purposes (Romans 12:1–2).

Such people will not care about how people see them, or their reputation. Their primary focus will be to progressively incarnate Christ's love in their lives as a witness to those around them of His love for them and, in doing so, to see others won for Him.

This of course does not mean that we then try to meet every need that we see around us; if we do that, we will burn ourselves out. But it does mean that our approach to life becomes much more intentional, that we prayerfully consider how we should use our resources, and that we ask God to give us the wisdom that we need to know how to spend our time, our abilities, and such like, so that they are not just used haphazardly, but for the glory of God. Obviously this does not mean that we do not have times of relaxation, or that we stop having fun; again if we did that, we would just burn ourselves out. But, for example, if we have been inclined to spend four hours every night playing computer games we might talk to God about perhaps using some of that time for other things!

However, having a servant heart is not just about having the right attitude to our own life or even being without prejudice, as these words spoken by Jesus show us:

> *Whoever does not bear his cross and come after Me cannot be My disciple. For which of you, intending to build a tower, does not sit down first and count the cost, whether he has enough to finish it – lest, after he has laid the foundation, and is not able to finish, all who see it begin to mock him, saying, 'This man began to build and was not able to finish' ... So likewise, whoever of you does not forsake all that he has cannot be My disciple.*
>
> (Luke 14:27–30, 33 NKJV)

Having looked at the context and other similar passages, what I understand Jesus to be saying is not that we literally have to leave everything, although for some of us it might come to that, but that we need to surrender our desires, our agendas, and our plans to God, so that we are no longer in the driving seat of our lives; He is. The Lord may then either give them back to us, or perhaps give us something else instead.

I must admit that I have found this chapter personally

challenging and I find myself wondering whether I have explained things particularly well, but it is a difficult spiritual principle to grasp and to explain. You may want not only to pray about it, but also perhaps to do some further reading. Assuming you can still get hold of it, I would like to recommend reading *The Grace of Yielding* by Derek Prince.

As I come to the end of this chapter let me remind you that Jesus also said:

> *Take My yoke upon you and learn from Me, for I am gentle and lowly in heart, and you will find rest for your souls. For My yoke is easy and My burden is light.*
>
> (Matthew 1:29–30 NKJV)

To me, what that means is that whilst we are called to progressively surrender our lives to God, as we do so, life becomes easier because we have put it all into His hands. I do not think that He ever intended us to be weighed down by what I call 'the cares of life'. More than that, I am certain that the more surrendered we are to Him, the more we will experience the kind of life that Jesus promised us (John 14:12).

# 13

# SINCERE LOVE

*Love must be sincere. Hate what is evil; cling to what is good. Be devoted to one another in brotherly love. Honour one another above yourselves. Never be lacking in zeal, but keep your spiritual fervour, serving the Lord. Be joyful in hope, patient in affliction, faithful in prayer. Share with God's people who are in need. Practise hospitality.*

(Romans 12:9–13)

The above verses show us once again that there is a clear link between our relationship with God and how we relate to each other; between the spiritual and the natural. This indicates that there is no distinction between them in God's eyes, and yet in the world in which we live people have a tendency to live their lives in compartments.

This speaks to me about the fragmented nature of lives lived in a fallen world (Genesis 3:1–24). God starts to heal this in us as we partner with Him, and in doing so He enables us to love Him and others as well as ourselves, more and more fully as He heals and restores our lives.

The sincere love spoken of in the verses quoted is thus very much rooted in our relationship with God. John makes this even plainer than is perhaps the case with the quote from Romans at the beginning of this chapter, and also plainer than I did in the first chapter of this book:

> *We love because he first loved us. If anyone says, 'I love God,' yet hates his brother, he is a liar. For anyone who does not love his brother, whom he has seen, cannot love God, whom he has not seen. And he has given us this command: Whoever loves God must also love his brother.*
>
> (1 John 4:19–21)

In my first chapter I spoke also of the *practical* nature of the love that we are to have for each other (1 John 3:16–18), and that connection is evident again in the verses from Romans that we are discussing here, as we are encouraged not only to practise hospitality but also to help those in need within the family of God.

For me, hospitality is not about offering someone a meal or a bed for the night, although that may well be part of what we do for those who are members of the family of God, as well as possibly those who are not, but is about an attitude of heart that makes people feel welcome, whether it is to our home or to our church. It is about a willingness to love others and to share our lives with them for a moment or even for a lifetime, depending on the nature of our relationship with them.

When we welcome people into our lives, homes and churches, it is a powerful witness to the reality and love of God; it will change people's lives and may well be a stepping stone to healing for them, or even result in them making a commitment to

Christ. Certainly it was a vital part of the healing that I have experienced over the last five or six years, as well as being the key to my conversion in 1986.

I became a Christian as a result of going on holiday with a group from a friend's church. The love and the care that these believers showed me, even when I swore and shouted at them, pointed me towards God in a way that nothing else would have done. Even now I can vividly remember certain things that happened on that holiday that touched my heart – kindnesses that were shown to me that had such an impact on me that the only response I could make was to open my heart to Jesus.

When it comes to helping people, it is worth remembering that Jesus spoke on a number of occasions about this throughout what I call His 'ministry years' (Matthew 6:1–4). Also, on two occasions He miraculously multiplied a small quantity of food in order to feed thousands of people, because they were hungry (Matthew 14:13–21; 15:29–39), thus modelling to us how to love one another in a practical way.

Perhaps here I should say that whilst we may not experience a miraculous multiplication of our resources, if we pool them we can make a difference, as can be seen from the many churches that are doing so by running projects for the homeless and food banks for people in need. However, even when churches are running such social action projects, there can be a certain amount of blindness within a congregation, even perhaps an unwillingness, to recognise the needs of those in their midst who are in need of some kind of help and support.

Sadly, I have heard of people asking for help from their church and being made to feel bad for having done so. This is not only unkind but also unloving. I am not suggesting that we should necessarily always help others; we may not be able to do so for all sorts of reasons, but no one should be made to feel that it is wrong to ask for help.

Personally, I think that all churches need to build a list of contacts within different agencies, organisations and charities that can provide support and help to those in need, so that those whom the church is unable to help can be referred on to someone who may be able to do so.

Having said that, perhaps I should add here that there are a number of different ways in which we can show our love for one another, but, whatever we do, we must not make people feel that they are part of some kind of 'care system' or that they are a project of some kind. Whatever we do needs to reflect the fact that we are all individuals. There is no 'one-size-fits-all' approach to what I call 'family life'.

One of the churches that I was part of years ago had what was called a 'Dorcas box' into which people put food contributions during the course of a month, and then it was given to the person/family that was struggling financially the most within the congregation.

One month I was given it and I was not sure how to take it at all; whilst I appreciated the gesture, I also felt very uncomfortable about it! I look back now and think that I would have felt less uncomfortable about it if it had been done less publicly, but it certainly touched my heart and I still feel a lot of gratitude about it even now.

The scripture shared at the beginning of the chapter speaks not only about being devoted to one another in brotherly love, but also about honouring each other, and it seems to me that what this means for us in practice is summed up in Philippians chapter 2:

> *Do nothing out of selfish ambition or vain conceit, but in humility consider others better than yourselves. Each of you should look not only to your own interests, but also to the interests of others.*
>
> (Philippians 2:3–4)

Another aspect of loving one another flows out of grace, which is often described as being 'God's riches at Christ's expense', but whilst that all sounds very clever it does not give us the understanding that we need to incorporate it into our lives to any great extent. To me a far better definition is that grace is 'the gift of acceptance until we become acceptable'.

Having reached this point in the chapter I am sure that some of you are saying that what I have been talking about is very difficult to do, that you just do not have the time, or even perhaps that the church that you belong to is too big, so that what I have been saying is impossible to do. But that, in a sense, is the point. We cannot live the way God wants us to in our own strength, but only in His; we need to live our lives in partnership with the Holy Spirit, who will progressively transform us and equip us to live in the way that Jesus called us to.

# 14

# THE BOND OF PEACE

*I, therefore, the prisoner of the Lord, beseech you to walk wor-*
*thy of the calling with which you were called, with all lowliness*
*and gentleness, with long-suffering, bearing with one another*
*in love, endeavouring to keep the unity of the Spirit in the*
*bond of peace.*
(Ephesians 4:1–3 NKJV)

The first thought that went through my head as I looked at these verses from Ephesians was that a lot of people think that unity is about uniformity and conformity, but for us as Christians, that cannot possibly be the case; otherwise it would mean that God wants us to become clones of each other and of Jesus. The basis for us to come together in unity cannot be based, for example, upon us all agreeing on what we believe, because we are all at different stages in our faith journey; nor can it be built on our core values, and for that same reason. So for me, what we need to do is to look at how we should deal with our differences in a Biblical way and what we should do about them when they become an issue.

I was talking to someone recently about some theological issues that we do not agree on, when we both suddenly realised that the core issue is in fact how we see the Bible. Since we are not able to agree on that, we both came to the conclusion that we would just have to agree to differ on the issues in question; otherwise we would end up completely breaking the bond of peace, which would ultimately mean that our friendship would come to an end.

In some situations involving conflict, particularly those like the one I have just described, the key to it will be to learn how to disagree agreeably, which is not a skill that any of us acquire overnight. But in other more personal situations, there may well be a process involved before the bond of peace can be fully restored. In His teaching Jesus gave us an example of such a process that is incredibly practical and that I think we should use in such situations. Let's now look at it briefly.

The teaching in question can be found in Matthew's Gospel:

*If your brother sins against you, go and tell him his fault between you and him alone. If he hears you, you have gained your brother. But if he will not hear, take with you one or two more, that 'by the mouth of two or three witnesses every word may be established.' And if he refuses to hear them, tell it to the church. But if he refuses to even hear the church, let him be to you like a heathen and a tax collector.*

(Matthew 18:15–17 NKJV)

Obviously the teaching needs a little unpacking as there are other factors that come into play when putting this into practice.

These require some thought, starting with what I am going to call 'stage one' of the process.

In stage one, Jesus advocates speaking to the person alone, but this may not always be appropriate. I would suggest that where abuse and/or violence has taken place it would be wiser to go straight to the next stage, perhaps even bringing someone in to mediate in the proposed meeting, assuming that you can find someone who is willing to do so and that the other person is in agreement with you involving that person.

Another factor that needs to be considered is where you are going to meet. Finding some 'neutral ground' might be best, perhaps even somewhere public like a coffee shop, but a lot will depend on the issues involved; if they are of a personal nature a home belonging to a third party might well be a better venue.

When it comes to the second stage it is important to choose not only the venue carefully, but also who is to go with you; your two best friends may not necessarily be the right people to take with you, particularly if they have had issues with the person that you are going to speak to! It may also be appropriate to have an older couple there rather than two singles, but that depends on the circumstances and the issues involved.

The final stage of the process, which is generally interpreted as speaking to the leadership about the issues that you are having with the individual in question, should not be taken lightly; it should only be done after much thought and prayer, as of course should the whole process.

It is vital to remember all the way through this process that you are working towards reconciliation and the restoration of the relationship in question. Any other agenda will end up causing further strife and perhaps even division, so before you start doing anything, I would suggest that you work things through with God first.

Whenever I have issues with people, I go to God and give Him the situation, as I want Him to be at the centre of whatever happens in that situation in the future. I then work through anything that I did wrong and ask His forgiveness before I begin looking at forgiving the other person, or people, involved. This is because I know that forgiveness is the key to healing (Matthew 18:21–35) and recognise that when I have been 'wounded', God is the only one who can heal me.

Perhaps here I should say that working through forgiveness involves an act of our will. More than that, it is a decision that we make in obedience to the teachings of Jesus, recognising that doing so allows God to come into the situation and work out His purpose in it.

Walking in forgiveness is a vital part of building and maintaining a healthy community life. If we do not do this, we will create all sorts of problems, not only for ourselves but also for those around us (Hebrews 12:14–15).

The verses given at the beginning of this chapter also speak of 'bearing with one another in love'. There are always going to be people whom we find difficult, but we are told in the book of Proverbs that:

> *As iron sharpens iron,*
> *So a man sharpens the countenance of his friend.*
>
> (Proverbs 27:17 NKJV)

To clarify things a bit, let me put what this proverb is saying into other words: the sea swirls the pebbles around on the beach, thus over the course of time smoothing off their rough edges, and the same thing will happen as we live together in community – God will use our interaction with one another to change us, to make us more like Christ.

Being part of such a diverse family as the Church is not always going to be easy, but the rewards of community life make it worthwhile: we end up having relationships with people we might not otherwise have met and having a variety of experiences that will enable our growth not only as individuals but also as a community, as well as enriching our lives.

In Part 3 of this book, 'The internal structure and the roof', we will be looking at leadership, vision and discipleship. These are aspects of church life that are rarely talked about these days, yet they are vital to the spiritual health of the Church.

# PART 3

# THE INTERNAL STRUCTURE AND THE ROOF

# 15

# THE STRUCTURE OF
# LEADERSHIP

*Paul and Barnabas appointed elders for them in each church
and, with prayer and fasting, committed them to the Lord, in
whom they had put their trust.*

(Acts 14:23)

From this verse we see that Paul and Barnabas were involved in the appointment of 'elders', also known as 'bishops' and 'overseers' in some translations, in the new churches, some of which would have been planted by these individuals. But there are also a number of other words used to refer to leaders, as studying the New Testament makes plain. Biblically, the role of elders involves things like shepherding the flock (1 Peter 5:2–3) and teaching (1 Timothy 3:2–5).

Paul was an apostle, which is one of the five leadership offices referred to by many as the 'fivefold ministry' (see Ephesians 5:11–13). I will now briefly define these five offices before I look at one final leadership role.

Let me begin by speaking about the role of apostles. The

word 'apostle' comes from the Greek word *apostolos* and means 'a sent one'. Their role can involve:

- planting churches (Acts implies this at various points)
- building spiritual foundations in the Church (1 Corinthians 3:10–11)
- teaching (Acts 2:42)
- testifying about Jesus and what He did through His life, death and resurrection (Acts 4:33; 5:42)
- exhorting and encouraging other leaders.

More than that, they should recognise the call of God on their life to be an apostle (1 Corinthians 9:1–2), as well as having signs, wonders and miracles following their ministry (2 Corinthians 12:12).

The prophet's role is described to some extent by the meaning of the word 'prophet', which comes from the Greek word *prophetes*, meaning 'one who speaks forth, who divulges or makes known, a proclaimer of the divine revelation'. Their role involves:

- (like apostles) building spiritual foundations (Ephesians 2:20)
- sharing words of knowledge and of wisdom, along with prophetic words
- bringing not only words of exhortation, edification and encouragement, but also messages of direction and correction.

Their ministry, again like that of apostles, will be accompanied by signs, wonders and miracles.

Before moving on to talk about the role of the evangelist, I think I need to say that there is a big difference between prophets and those who use the gift of prophecy (1 Corinthians 12:7–11) as there has been a lot of confusion about this. The first is a leadership role, whilst the second is not; moreover this principle applies to other ministries and gifts.

The word 'evangelist' comes from the Greek word *euangelistes*, which literally means 'a messenger of good'. In Christian terms this denotes a communicator of the gospel, sometimes referred as the 'good news' of the Kingdom, and that encapsulates for us their role amongst us.

A true evangelist will have a heart for the lost, for those who do not know peace with God and need to be shown the way of salvation, and will spend a large portion of their time reaching out to such people in one way or another.

Whilst every Christian is called to witness, to win the lost (Matthew 28:18–20), evangelists have a particular gift in this area. Their proclamation of the gospel will be accompanied by signs, wonders and miracles (Acts 8:5–7); the same is true of all five offices, in fact all Biblical leadership roles.

Evangelists will also know the Word of God and will use it not only to motivate other believers to witness, but also to train them how to do so, either formally or informally.

It is from the Greek word *poimen* that we get the word 'pastor', and that means 'a shepherd or one who tends flocks and herds'. Basically, pastors are the ones who ensure that the care that is needed for everyone within the community is provided, whether they do it themselves or delegate it to others, but I will say more about this in a later chapter.

Some Christians believe that the roles of pastor and teacher are actually one role, but I disagree, partly because if it was just one role there would be no need to use two labels for it and partly because I know of individuals who function in only one of the roles.

The word 'teacher' comes from the Greek word *didaskalos*, meaning 'one who instructs', and since all of us have some understanding of what a teacher's role entails, I will move on to speak about the role of deacons.

Having briefly outlined what is often referred to as the fivefold ministry, I would like to say that I think it is probable that 'elder' may be another word for 'pastor', because not only are the roles similar, but also pastors are not mentioned anywhere in Acts.

It is also possible that 'elder' may even be a generic term that covers all of the fivefold ministries. Looking at Peter (1 Peter 5:1) and other leaders in the New Testament suggests that could be the case, but it is hard to be certain about it.

Perhaps I should say here too that a deacon is in fact a servant of the Church and, whilst in some church circles the role is seen as a leadership role, I am not sure that this is what the Bible teaches, because their title comes from the Greek word *diakonos* which means 'one who serves'. Deacons are usually those who take care of the more practical aspects of church life (Acts 6:1–7), but they may go on to do other things, as both Stephen (Acts 6:8–10) and Philip did.

However, whilst the New Testament teaches us that there is a variety of different roles, a large part of the Church of today either fails to recognise some of them, or even changes the job descriptions around. For example, in some parts of the Church, deacons function like Biblical elders and vice versa. Not only that; in some parts of the Church, pastors are expected to fulfil some of the other Biblical leadership roles too, and other roles are not necessarily seen as being relevant for today. So leadership in churches today generally looks rather different from what the Bible teaches.

However, the most significant change from the Biblical model of leadership is the idea in some church circles that a pastor is more like the manager of a business, a CEO, than a shepherd. In such a model the Church is seen, although perhaps not explicitly, as an organisation rather than as a family, which means that relationships become rather impersonal. This can result in people's needs being ignored, or, even worse, people being treated as if it is wrong for them to have needs at all.

For me the bottom line is that the hallmark of our lives as Christians is meant to be love, whether we are talking about us as individuals or in a corporate sense. Therefore, whatever model of leadership is being used should reflect that, along with the range and diversity of roles that the Bible describes.

Not only that; I think there also needs to be a recognition that whatever title is given to a leader, that person should play to their strengths, rather than being expected to be a 'Jack of all trades'. They should be able to delegate the things that are outside their abilities and gifts, rather than perhaps spreading themselves so thin that none of what they do is done particularly well, either because they are asking too much of themselves – or because others are.

Finally, I think it is vital that wherever it is practical and possible, a church has a leadership *team* rather than one person as the only leader. This should ensure that all aspects of leadership are covered and it should also ensure that leaders do not burn themselves out.

# 16

# THE QUALIFICATIONS FOR LEADERSHIP

*This is a faithful saying: If a man desires the position of a bishop, he desires a good work. A bishop then must be blameless, the husband of one wife, temperate, sober-minded, of good behaviour, hospitable, able to teach; not given to wine, not violent, not greedy for money, but gentle, not quarrelsome, not covetous; one who rules his own house well, having his children in submission with all reverence …*

(1 Timothy 3:1–4 NKJV)

As I was reading the above quotation, I found myself focusing on the bit about a bishop being a 'husband of one wife'. This is where I could go off at a tangent, but I am not going to do that because the focus in this book is primarily on what the Bible says about community life.

From things that I have said in other parts of this book it is probably apparent that I do not see a problem with women being elders, or holding other leadership roles. But apart from that, having looked carefully at all the relevant scriptures, I see no other possibilities, or interpretations, for what the Bible says on this issue with regard to the subject of marriage and gender, so am not going to discuss it further as to do so would take me outside the scope of this book.

Underpinning that particular fragment of the quotation are the personal qualities of commitment and loyalty. In fact, much of this passage is about the character of the person who is going to perhaps be appointed to a leadership role.

The rest of the quotation speaks about qualities like being dependable, reliable, even-tempered and kind, and about being a good father. To me the passage describes someone who has reached a reasonable level of maturity in their life with God. It seems to me that they should be at a point in their lives where their walk and their talk are no longer poles apart; where many of their 'rough edges' have been smoothed off and their life reflects Christ in such a way that those around them can see something of Him in them.

In today's Church there is still far too much emphasis on a person's formal training and age when new leaders are being chosen, whereas Biblically the focus is on other things; for example, character and behaviour. These are not, generally, things that those who are young in age, or in faith, have yet developed to the degree that perhaps the passage suggests is required for leaders.

Not only that; older people are all too often overlooked and yet their experience of life could potentially have prepared them to be exceptional leaders, assuming of course they are people whose character and behaviour reflect Christ in the way that I described earlier.

Such older people would probably have the maturity to deal

with situations that younger people might not be able to handle so well.

However, one of the biggest things that seems to be missing today in the understanding of what qualifies people for leadership is the ability to move in the power of the Spirit, and yet it is clear from Scripture that that is part of all leadership roles.

If you want to look into this aspect further, there are plenty of Biblical examples to look at. Here are just a few to get you started:

- Peter and the healing of a beggar (Acts 3:1–9)
- Peter and the dishonest couple (Acts 5:1–11)
- The apostles and the healing of many (Acts 5:12–16)
- Philip and the miraculous (Acts 8:5–8)
- The miraculous conversion experience of Saul (Acts 9:1–18), who later became known as Paul.

It seems to me that leaders are meant to model how to operate in the supernatural to those under their care, so that ultimately anyone in their congregation who wants to learns how to do so is able to do so. To put it another way, it should be progressively natural for each one of us to move in the supernatural; doing so is not just the prerogative of the few, but something that we can all be equipped for.

Today there are all too many people in leadership roles who do not ever seem to move in the supernatural and I think that for some of them at least the issue may be that God has not called them to do whatever it is that they are doing. They may see being in ministry as a career, rather than as a calling, but I believe that the Bible teaches us that 'God qualifies the called'. See for example John 21:15–17, which speaks about the reinstatement of Peter's call after he had betrayed Jesus; another example is Paul's 'Damascus Road' experience that I mentioned earlier.

A leader who knows the call of God upon their life will progressively develop the heart of a servant; they will recognise that that is what their call entails. Paul, for example, although he could have asked people to support him financially never did so, preferring instead to make tents for a living (Acts 18:1–3; 20:34) rather than being a potential burden to the Church, and he did that because that was part of the way in which he felt that God had called him to serve 'the Body'.

The ultimate example of a servant-hearted leader is of course Jesus Himself who, as has already been mentioned, washed His disciples' feet (John 13:1–17), and note what He says about Himself as a servant towards the end of his teaching in Mark 10:42–45 (see v. 45). His teaching and life should be the model for all leaders.

However, the hallmark of a true leader is not just their willingness to serve but also the way in which they use their authority (1 Peter 5:2–3). If it is expressed as if they are superior to those under their care, or in a controlling way, such as would be the case in a dictatorship, or even perhaps in a business, then that is not only what is described as lording it over people, but is also ungodly.

A truly Godly leader will use his or her authority in the context of us being a family; it will come from relationship and therefore from 'the side', rather than from above. Furthermore, their ministry will be based on love and on Kingdom principles, and will be expressed in the power of the Spirit.

If a Godly leader has to discipline someone in the church

over something, they will spend as much time as is necessary talking and praying with them about the issue in question. Any action that is taken will be done in love, having worked things through as far as possible with the person in a loving way, and only after having sought the Lord about the right path to take in the situation in question.

The ultimate goal in any disciplinary situation should always be the restoration of the person, not their punishment. Excluding them from the community not only should be a last resort, but also should never be seen as a permanent thing, as studying1 Corinthians 5:1–5 and 2 Corinthians 2:5–11 will indicate.

I think that it is important at this point to make you aware, if you are not already, that in some church circles Biblical church discipline has been replaced by a form of behaviour modification that was originally intended for use by trained therapists in residential centres. From my perspective, such a programme is not only unbiblical but also a highly dangerous development, as I think that anyone going through it is going to be damaged by the process that is used, although it may not necessarily show until some years down the road.

Whatever issues a person has, it is only God who has the answer and it is to Him that leaders need to look, not psychological remedies created by people whose knowledge and understanding is limited to say the least. More than that, He is the source of all inner transformation and healing.

# 17

# SHEPHERDING THE FLOCK

*To the elders among you, I appeal as a fellow-elder, a witness of Christ's sufferings and one who also will share in the glory to be revealed: Be shepherds of God's flock that is under your care, serving as overseers – not because you must, but because you are willing, as God wants you to be; not greedy for money, but eager to serve; not lording it over those entrusted to you, but being examples to the flock.*

(1 Peter 5:1–3)

A s you can see from both the title of this chapter and the quotation that I have shared, I am going to talk about shepherding the flock in this chapter, but before I do so I think it is important for me to tell you, if you do not already know of course, that shepherds in the Middle East go in front of their flock and lead them, rather than driving them from behind as shepherds do here in the UK. This is of great importance since Jesus would have known this when He spoke about the Shepherd and His flock; hence Him saying:

*He calls his own sheep by name and leads them out. When he has brought out all his own, he goes on ahead of them, and his sheep follow him because they know his voice.* *(John 10:3b–4)*

From this quotation we can see that the good Shepherd knows His sheep and they know him; as a result they have built a relationship with Him that is based on trust. The same should apply with regard to leaders and those God has placed in their care; elders/pastors need to get to know the members of their congregation and in turn let the people get to know them, as we are all part of the same family.

Perhaps here I should say that I do realise that in a big church this is something that no one person can possibly do. But, with a good team, strategies can be developed to ensure that people become connected to a particular leader who is then responsible for their pastoral care.

Knowing the members of their congregation will enable pastors to be able to discern the different seasons in people's lives so they will be able to encourage them to take 'time out' when it is needed, or even to grow and develop at the right time. Moreover, they will be able to recognise the times when people are struggling and therefore in need of some extra care and support.

The shepherd prepares the way for the sheep and they know that he has done that because he leads them from the front, rather than driving them from behind. Pastors need to do the same; they cannot expect the congregation to do something or to go somewhere they are not prepared to go themselves.

Further on in the same teaching from John's Gospel that I quoted from previously, we read:

> *I am the good shepherd. The good shepherd lays down his life for the sheep.*
>
> (John 10:11)

This verse can be seen in different two ways; it speaks not only of the servant heart that we should all have, but also of the very real possibility that pastors may have to give up their own lives in order to protect members of their congregation.

Going back to that same passage in John, the next couple of verses show clearly the difference between those who are true shepherds and those who are not:

> *The hired hand is not the shepherd who owns the sheep. So when he sees the wolf coming, he abandons the sheep and runs away. Then the wolf attacks the flock and scatters it. The man runs away because he is a hired hand and cares nothing for the sheep.*
>
> (John 10:12–13)

From the two verses that I have just quoted we can see the contrast between those who are doing pastoral work as a career and those who have been called by God to do it. The commitment that comes with the knowledge of being called will lead such pastors not only to be fully committed to the well-being of their flock, but also to be more willing to fight for members of their congregation in prayer when needed.

Let me develop the shepherd analogy further by looking at some other things that shepherds do. They:

- feed their sheep, leading them from one field to another as the need arises
- comfort their sheep when they need to
- direct their sheep
- work to restore them when necessary.

From this list of additional tasks we can see that it is part of a pastor's role to teach those under their care, as well as providing encouragement and counselling to them. Not only that; the pastoral task involves working for the restoration of those God has placed under their care.

A good shepherd can be recognised by the way in which the sheep gather to him, and the same is true of a true pastor; the members of their congregation will gather to them willingly because they are incarnating the love of Christ in their lives.

However, bad shepherding can result in the sheep being scattered. This was the case in the days of Ezekiel with regard to the shepherds of Israel, as can be seen in Ezekiel's prophecy that speaks about shepherds and sheep.

Ezekiel 34:1–16 has a number of keys for understanding the nature of pastoral ministry, but what I particularly want to focus on are the things that the shepherds of Israel had failed to do. Ezekiel states these at the beginning of the prophecy. They had:

- failed to take care of the flock (vv. 1–3)
- not strengthened the weak or healed the sick (v. 4a)
- not brought back the strays or looked for the lost (v. 4b)
- ruled the flock harshly (v. 4c).

It was these things that had caused the flock to become scattered.

Looking at this list in the light of what I have already spoken about, we can see that there are some things we can add to it. It is the second to last point that I want to now briefly discuss.

Over the years that I have been a Christian I have sadly seen a number of people who have left the church that I was part of. Their faith has taken a beating for one reason or another, but sadly, all too often there has been no follow-up by the leadership, although there may have been contact made by members of the congregation.

Many of these people have been hurt by the Church, by the family of God, and had the leadership been involved then perhaps they would have come home again. If you are like me, you will have a heart to see the prodigals return, but they are probably not going to do so unless people reach out in love to them.

Let me finish this chapter by saying that pastors are meant to care for God's family as well as, if not better than, they would their own. If they would not deal with one of their children as they are dealing with one of God's, then there is something wrong somewhere. Love enables people to position themselves in God for all that He wants to give them.

# 18

# WORKING TOGETHER

*Who then is Paul, and who is Apollos, but ministers through whom you believed, as the Lord gave to each one? I planted, Apollos watered, but God gave the increase. So then neither he who plants is anything, nor he who waters, but God who gives the increase. Now he who plants and he who waters are one, and each one will receive his own reward according to his own labour. For we are God's fellow workers; you are God's field, you are God's building.*

(1 Corinthians 3:5–9 NKJV)

In this quotation we see a small picture of what it looks like to work together to further the Kingdom. The analogy used is one of planting and watering, done by Paul and Apollos working in partnership with each other and with God, who is the one who multiplies the crop that is to be reaped. Whatever field we are working in, whether it is to do with our own lives or other people's lives, we are called to work together and in partnership with God; hence the way in which God speaks about:

- the 'Priesthood of all believers'
- the 'Building'

- the 'Body' of Christ
- the 'Army' of the Lord
- the 'Bride' of Christ.

All of these are pictures that illustrate co-operation in important different ways.

However, before we can work together, we need to understand what it is that God wants us to do and recognise that the basis for doing so is Jesus, rather than complete harmony of thought or belief. All ministry flows out of love, is built on Kingdom principles and is done in partnership with the Holy Spirit. This applies to everyone, whether they are in leadership or not; leaders, however, carry the ultimate responsibility before God for all ministry taking place under their covering.

In Exodus 18:13–26 we are told that Jethro spoke to Moses about the need for a team of people to help him deal with people's disputes. This story has a lot to teach us about the principles involved in raising people up into roles within the life of the church. We can see that delegating some aspects of the work will:

- lighten the load for the leader
- enable them to focus on the things that for one reason or another they need to do personally
- give them time to focus on the things that they are not able to delegate
- stop them from perhaps burning themselves out.

When leaders delegate something of their authority to others, they need to be able to keep those people accountable for their actions and words, which is why they need to seek God before appointing people into 'ministry roles'. Just because someone appears to have the right character, gifting, availability and willingness does not make them the right person to fulfil the role that is on offer.

I would say that even if there is clear evidence that the person in question is already beginning to operate in that role, leaders still need to hear from God because timing can sometimes be the issue. Raising someone up into a role that they are not yet ready for can be, and generally is, extremely damaging for the person involved; sadly, I have witnessed the consequences of such decisions over the years.

If someone is to be given a role in the church then another vital aspect is that, whilst there should be one person who has the final say on things, there should also be a team around that person who have an input into those decisions in some way. This is because such decisions are too important to be left to one person; he or she could be pressured into putting someone into a role that they are not ready for, or even into putting their friends into key roles, so leaders need to have at least one other person involved who will help to keep them from making such mistakes.

Another vital aspect of delegation is of course recognising that there may be a need to provide training to whoever is given the role. For example: if someone is being appointed to a 'technical role', such as looking after the sound equipment, they may need to do a course on maintaining it if their knowledge is too basic.

It is particularly vital that the main leader of a church chooses the right people for his/her leadership team. Such teams need to involve people with different gifts and abilities, as well as individuals from different backgrounds and age-groups, because having a team of people who are too similar will almost certainly be detrimental to the life of the church in all sorts of ways.

Prayer will of course be the biggest key to making good choices, but leaders should not be surprised if God starts speaking to them about some unlikely people! All the way through the Bible, we see that God's choices of people He wants to use can be quite surprising. A good example of this can be seen in 1 Samuel 16:1–13, which is the story of how God tells Samuel to go and anoint one of Jesse's sons as the king in place of Saul (1 Samuel 13:14). The one that Samuel ends up anointing is not the one that he thought it was going to be, but the youngest son, David, who is the only person in the Bible to be described as having a heart after God's own heart.

God looks at the heart, as is made plain to us in 1 Samuel 16:7 and in other places in the Bible. The heart is described as being 'the wellspring of life' in Proverbs 4:23, whilst Jesus says that:

*What comes out of a man, that defiles a man. For from within, out of the heart of men, proceed evil thoughts, adulteries, fornications, murders, thefts, covetousness, wickedness, deceit, lewdness, an evil eye, blasphemy, pride, foolishness. All these things come from within and defile a man.*

(Mark 7:20–23 NKJV)

It is therefore essential that leaders do not rely solely on what they see, or even hear, about certain people, but instead ask God for discernment with regard to their interaction with people, particularly when it comes to choosing other leaders, or when filling other ministry roles within the life of the church. The gift of discernment is not the same thing as natural discernment and seems to have largely fallen into disuse, yet it is an essential part of building a healthy spiritual life, not only for us as individuals but also for our well-being on a corporate level.

Perhaps here the point that needs to be made is that the 'supernatural', things such as the gifts of the Spirit, should be seen as being part and parcel of our lives, both individually and corporately. We should have an expectation that God will show up in all sorts of wonderful and exciting ways just as He did in the life of the early Church. The book of Acts is full of stories of His intervention in people's lives in different ways.

Having spoken, albeit briefly, about the need to delegate and of the importance of team ministry, let me now mention the need for leaders of churches to gather their congregations together, to socialise and pray together, as well as combining forces to work on joint projects. Things such as shelters for the homeless, food banks and after-school clubs are the sort of thing I am particularly thinking of, but joint celebrations can also be a great way to bring different groups of Christians together.

Such things can be good vehicles for people to see the love that we have for one another regardless of what differentiates us. They can be an amazing witness, to those who do not yet know Christ, of the love of God operating through His people.

# 19

# THE VALUE OF VISION

*Where there is no revelation, the people cast off restraint; but blessed is he who keeps the law.*
(Proverbs 29:18)

Vision is an essential part of our lives as Christians, not just for us as individuals but also for us on a corporate level. It provides hope and purpose, and gives us the motivation that we need to keep on seeking God for His heart for us.

All the key characters in the Bible were given some kind of vision for their lives which caused them to change direction. Let us look at a few briefly:

- Abram, whom God later renamed Abraham (Genesis 17:5), was told to leave his country and go where God led him – to a new land (Genesis 12:1–2); interestingly he was told that God would bless not only him but also 'all peoples on earth' (v. 3), which incidentally was undoubtedly a prophecy about the coming of Jesus (Matthew 1:1–16) who is of course the one who brought that promise into being.

- Noah was sent to Nineveh to call the people to repentance (Jonah 1:1–2); he tried to run away from his call (Jonah 1:3) but in the end was not able to do so, and fulfilled it (Jonah 3:1–5).

- Jeremiah was called (Jeremiah 1:4–5) to be 'a prophet to the nations' (v. 5), but it is worth noting that his appointment was made even before he was born.

- Paul was 'an apostle of Christ Jesus by the will of God' (Ephesians 1:1); he started out his Christian life preaching the gospel to the Jews, but eventually changed direction and preached to a variety of different people-groups, planting churches wherever he went.

The Bible is quite clear that God has a plan and a purpose for each of our lives (Jeremiah 29:11), which is confirmed by Ephesians 2:10; discovering and fulfilling it is an important part of our journey into God's heart for us.

Sadly, all too many Christians today fail to recognise the truth of this, often because they have reduced their faith to what happened at the time of conversion. They are blind to the possibility of having an adventure with God that will lead them into a very much more fruitful life than they would have by continuing in the direction they are going in.

Discovering God's vision for our lives can be just as exciting as fulfilling it. God can speak to us personally as He did to Jeremiah (see Jeremiah 1:4–10), through dreams and visions, in a prophetic way as He did for David (1 Samuel 16:13) and in other ways, but whatever way He chooses there will always be some kind of confirmation.

Once we begin to get a revelation of God's purpose for us, we need to start praying for wisdom about the next step, and once that is achieved for the next, and so on, because we will not fulfil the vision without partnering with the Holy Spirit and following His leading.

Much of what I have said about the effect of God's vision for us as individuals also applies to corporate vision. It not only gives hope, purpose and motivation, but will also bring people together as they will unify around the goals contained within it and will take on board the core values that result from it if it is birthed in the right way.

Discovering God's vision for a church in my opinion is something that the whole church should be involved in, or if it is a very big church, other leaders, heads of departments/ministries and other key people in the congregation. This will enable all those who are part of that community 'to take ownership' of the vision and encourage them to get involved in its fulfilment.

Obviously the process of discovery starts with seeking and listening to God. It may well include multiple areas of church life and the birthing of new ministries, but whatever people believe that God is saying to them then needs to be prayed through by the leadership team as a whole.

The primary leader, or senior pastor, is the one who is ultimately accountable to God for the life of the church and those under his/her care, so whilst others have been involved in the process it does not mean that he/she should necessarily take their contributions on board. The final decision is always taken by the senior leader. The congregation should pray for God to give him or her the necessary wisdom and clarity to make the required decisions.

Once a decision has been made it needs be put into documentary form, along with the appropriate core values and goals, so that it can be shared with the church. Such a document should of course include any scriptures that are relevant, along with any relevant prophecies. After that, the key will be developing the right strategy through seeking and listening to the Lord, which is of course the responsibility of the leadership.

Obviously no vision is ever fixed in stone. Circumstances change, people leave the church and new ones come in, so there will need to be regular reviews of the statement. Also, as in every area of church life, there needs to be a recognition that we should be follow the leading of the Holy Spirit at all times.

One of the things that I have noticed over the years is that churches that are more relational find it easier to change direction than those that are less so. I think this is because relational churches are more of an organism than an organisation, so are able to adapt more easily when change comes.

Sadly, some church leaders do not see the value of the kind of process that I have been describing, and upon taking on the leadership of a new church will often try to duplicate the vision of their previous one, or even that of some other successful church, and as result will struggle to unify the church, because the congregation will have no sense of ownership of the vision.

This can lead to such leaders falling into 'the control trap', where they assume that uniformity and conformity will bring unity. This in turn can lead to them seeing those who do not fit their criteria as a problem, and treating them as such. Such a strategy not only results in people getting hurt and damaged but also creates a church that is far less able to fulfil its God-given destiny.

True unity comes from the heart – a person's love for God. It is not something that can be forced, but is the product of aligning oneself with God, which brings us into alignment with one another. It comes from having a leadership team whose members are seeking God's agenda rather than their own. The result is an abundance of creativity and diversity, of life, within the church, as the Holy Spirit then flows freely in the midst of us. That, in turn, will bring an explosion of the supernatural.

# 20

# THE IMPORTANCE OF DISCIPLESHIP

*And Jesus came and spoke to them, saying, 'All authority has been given to Me in heaven and on earth. Go therefore and make disciples of all the nations, baptizing them in the name of the Father and of the Son and of the Holy Spirit, teaching them to observe all things that I have commanded you; and lo, I am with you always, even to the end of the age.'*
(Matthew 28:18–20 NKJV)

Before we can go and teach others about anything, as Jesus tells us to in the above quotation, we need first to understand what we are talking about, as it is only in the place of understanding that we will be able to fulfil His commandment effectively.

It seems to me that for many of today's believers, discipleship is not on their radar. Some were undoubtedly burnt badly by what is generally referred to as 'the Heavy Shepherding Movement' of the 1960s to 1980s. Others perhaps do not see the need for discipleship, because they do not understand what it is, or they may even think it is about whatever is being communicated from the front of the church. Yet discipleship is an essential part of the Christian life, so I think that it is important to begin this chapter by briefly defining what I am talking about.

Let me start by looking at how Jesus discipled His followers. First He called them to follow Him (Matthew 9:9) and they then joined Him on the road, where they all lived as a community. Not only that; Jesus also spent time with them, teaching them about the Kingdom (Mark 4:10–12) and then modelling the truths that He was teaching them in His own life (Mark 8:1–9).

Basically, Jesus discipled people so that they would become established in their faith through understanding the principles of the Kingdom and learning how to incarnate them, and indeed Him – His character and love – in their lives.

Let me suggest to you that another way of looking at discipleship is to think about family life and how children's lives are shaped through it. Discipleship is God's way of providing that for His children. Being part of a church family is a messy business, as can be seen from what Paul says in his first letter to the church at Corinth, and also from the life of Peter, but part of discipleship is learning how to deal in a Godly way with the difficulties that life throws at us.

Peter is a case in point. Out of fear he denied being one of Jesus' disciples during the last couple of days of His life here on earth (John 18:15–27) and yet it was Peter who preached to a crowd of about three thousand people on the day of Pentecost (Acts 2:14–41).

According to the Bible, two things happened between those two events. The first was that after His resurrection Jesus reinstated Peter (John 21:15–19), and the second was that Peter was baptised in the Spirit on the day of Pentecost just before he preached the message that I referred to above (Acts 2:1–4). But that is obviously not the whole story, as he could have left the area after his denial and gone elsewhere to live, a place where no one would know about the way in which he had failed.

People are going to fail, or mess up, in various ways at points on their journey into God's heart for them, leaders included. It is how we deal with these situations that indicates the maturity of our faith and our love – the quality of our discipleship. We need to recognise that dealing with failure, both ours and other people's, is part of our training. Failure can be a stepping stone to change and growth or it can be a stone that trips us up; the choice is ours.

When people fail it is not our place to judge them (Luke 6:37–42), although there may be a need for correction or discipline. We are called to:

- forgive them
- love them
- seek reconciliation with them wherever and whenever possible
- work towards their restoration
- not reject them or permanently exclude them from our lives.

Obviously what I have just said applies on a general basis, so I do need to say that there are some situations that we can face (such as abuse) where reconciliation may not be particularly wise, but such situations are the exception rather than the rule.

After Jesus' resurrection and the outpouring of the Holy Spirit at Pentecost (Acts 2:1–41), His disciples changed the face of the then known world. They took the gospel to wherever they were led to go by God, and as a result their numbers multiplied greatly, which of course affected the culture and how people lived.

If we want to see our nation turned back to God then we need to do what Jesus did and disciple people, so that the family of God multiplies to the point where we are numerous enough to be able to impact every sphere of life here. This will result in progressive national transformation.

The problem that we face today is how to disciple people in a different culture and time, but I believe that God can give us strategies for doing so. For example:

- A pastor, or someone to whom he/she has delegated the responsibility, could meet with a group of, say, twelve people one Sunday a month for a year to spend time with them, teaching, sharing and enabling them. If an evening a month was also included, that would be a reasonable chunk of time to spend getting to know each other, praying for one another, and identifying the areas of ministry where God has equipped them.

- If those in the initial group(s) with leadership ability were then given groups of their own, then the whole church could be discipled in a fairly short space of time.

- The process could even be repeated every couple of years to ensure that people are growing and maturing in their faith and to ensure that those who are new to the faith are discipled too.

However, we need to learn from the mistakes of the past and not allow the discipling of people to become too structured, hierarchical or rigid. It needs to be done in an intentionally loving way, because that is what will produce growth and lead to people becoming actively involved in the life of the Kingdom, which after all is part of the purpose of discipleship in the first place.

Let me suggest that since every church has its own identity and purpose, the leadership of each one needs to develop their own strategy in partnership with the Holy Spirit for the discipleship of the people who form their congregation. Taking on someone else's programme could be detrimental to the life of that church because the person who put it together will have designed it for their particular church, which will undoubtedly have been very different.

In the last part of this book, 'Working the fields outside', I will talk more about what is involved in the 'going' part of Jesus' commandment to make disciples, as well as looking at some of the different ways we can do it. Going in obedience is the hallmark of someone whose life has been surrendered to God and who is a true disciple of Christ.

# PART 4

## WORKING THE FIELDS OUTSIDE

# 21

# GATHERING THE HARVEST IN

*Jesus went through all the towns and villages, teaching in their synagogues, preaching the good news of the kingdom and healing every disease and sickness. When he saw the crowds, he had compassion on them, because they were harassed and helpless, like sheep without a shepherd. Then he said to his disciples, 'The harvest is plentiful but the workers are few ...'*
(Matthew 9:35–37)

The above quotation describes Jesus as teaching and preaching the good news of the Kingdom, which is something I have spoken a lot about in this book, but perhaps it would be helpful to give a basic definition of 'the Kingdom' in order to ensure that we are all on the same page.

The Kingdom as I understand it is the reign and rule of God over this world and all that is in it. After 'the Fall' (Genesis 3:1–24), dominion passed from Adam to satan. Jesus came to take it back, and whilst that mission was successful (Romans 5:15–17), the work of restoration will not be completed until after His Second Coming (Revelation 21:1). So we live in a time when, although the Kingdom is here, it is not yet here fully.

The healings and miracles that Jesus did were signs pointing to the reality of the coming Kingdom. The same applies when any of us do the same, and that is one of the reasons why the supernatural is of such importance.

As can be seen from the quotation at the beginning of this chapter, Jesus' motivation for His ministry was compassion. All of us should feel as He did when we recognise that someone we know, or meet when we are out and about, is 'lost'. Our compassion should motivate us to want to tell those people about the Kingdom – about Jesus and God's love for us (John 3:16).

Whilst we are not all evangelists, we are all called to be witnesses and to share the good news. There are a number of different ways in which we can do this, some of which I now want to look at briefly.

Let me begin with the kind of approach described in the quotation from Matthew's Gospel above, which I would call 'evangelistic crusades'. These have been done with great effect in the UK in the past by people like Billy Graham and Morris Cerullo.

Whilst such an approach has worked in the past, I am not convinced that large crusades are nearly as successful in the UK now, because our culture has changed significantly in the last twenty years or so. However, people like Reinhard Bonnke have led thousands to Christ at their rallies in Africa.

What are referred to as 'open airs' also used to have a greater impact than they seem to now. In fact I used to be part of a team that held a monthly open-air gathering in a local market when I lived in London, and we used to attract quite a lot of people. It involved not only a time of worship and a brief gospel message, but also dancing, drama, a presentation with a sketch board, and testimonies. I used to thoroughly enjoy doing it and it did produce some fruit, although I must admit that I do not know exactly how much.

Having said that, I am not sure that the kind of outreaches that we did then are particularly effective now. I am happy to say that The Turning, which is another kind of open-air outreach, is producing a lot of fruit and not just in the UK but also beyond. Their approach is formulaic, but simple enough that children as young as six or seven are using it with great effect.

When I lived in London I was also involved in door knocking, which also bore some fruit. It could be a lot of fun if you had the right partner, but if you were posting literature through someone's door you had to be careful not to put your fingers right through the letterbox in case they had a dog! I have to admit that now I am not sure if such an approach is particularly effective. My experience tells me that it tends to close people down to the gospel rather than opening them up, but I could be wrong.

What is generally referred to as 'treasure hunting', on the other hand, opens people up to the gospel, because giving someone a word from God will generally bypass their mind and reach their heart. A story from the life of Jesus that I particularly love, and that illustrates the kind of thing I am taking about, is the one about the woman at the well. Jesus spoke into her life in such a way that it changed her, and as a result she became a witness to others (John 4:1–42).

Over the years there have been a variety of strategies involving the use of the prophetic, which have had varying levels of success. Studying the Gospel story I have just mentioned – the account of the woman at the well – can provide a number of keys for anyone wanting to learn more about witnessing in this way.

Another approach that opens people's hearts up to the gospel involves offering to pray for healing. There are a number of different ways that this is being done by different groups; Healing Rooms (JGLM) and Healing On The Streets (HOTS) are two such organisations.

As you can probably imagine, all the above strategies for preaching the gospel to people are only the tip of the iceberg. There are far more ways of doing things than those I have described here, and there is still room for more. People are not all the same, and one size does not fit all, so we need to be creative in our approach to reaching the lost.

From my perspective, the biggest keys to seeing people saved are of course prayer and love; these have to be behind all that we do to advance the Kingdom. This brings me on to the subject of what people generally call 'friendship evangelism', which sounds very positive. However, trying to lead our friends to Christ, or befriending people with that in mind, carries a lot of risks, particularly for those who are not secure in their identity in Christ.

If we are more committed to the friendship than in seeing that friend won to Christ then we will undoubtedly compromise our witness to maintain the relationship. We will condone things that we should not; keep silent when we should speak the truth in love; and take part in activities, or go to places, that as Christians we know are wrong.

We are called to live in the world but not to be of it (1 John 2:15–17), and that means that we need to live in such way that we are seen as being different from other people. This can make friendship evangelism a difficult road to travel, because those who do not know Christ will undoubtedly find some of the things that we stand for difficult to understand.

In the next and final chapter, I am going to look at another way that we can witness. This approach is often referred to as the 'social gospel', but from my perspective it is in fact the natural outworking of our faith in God (1 Peter 2:11–12).

# 22

# DOING GOOD

*You are the light of the world. A city that is set on a hill cannot be hidden. Nor do they light a lamp and put it under a basket, but on a lampstand, and it gives light to all who are in the house. Let your light shine before all men, that they may see your good works and glorify your Father in heaven.*
(Matthew 5:14–16 NKJV)

What this quotation makes plain is that how we live and what we do can make a difference in Kingdom terms. We can be a witness to the reality and truth of the good news by doing good, both inside the church community and outside (Galatians 6:9–10).

As I said at the end of the last chapter, doing good is a natural outworking of our faith. James puts it like this:

*Someone will say, 'You have faith, and I have works.' Show me your faith without your works, and I will show you my faith by my works.'*
(James 2:18 NKJV)

Doing good can be as simple as being willing to help someone who is blind across the road, or buying a homeless person a meal. It is something that we can do in the context of our everyday life, or we can be more intentional about it and volunteer to help with a community project of some kind.

Again we will not be able to do this without the partnership of the Holy Spirit. We need His counsel (John 14:16–17) and guidance (John 16:13–14) in every part of our lives, and this area is no exception. The Spirit is the one who knows us the best, so He is able to reveal to us, as individuals, what we have been equipped to do, our gifts and abilities, as well as being able to show us how to use the things we have identified.

Whilst our works will not save us, they are the evidence of the faith that we claim to have (James 2:17) and as such are part of a normal Christian life. In fact Jesus had quite a lot to say about the way in which His true followers would live, the parable of the sheep and the goats (Matthew 25:31–46) being just one strand of His teaching on this subject.

In that parable, which is primarily about judgement, Jesus speaks of:

- feeding the hungry
- giving water to those who were thirsty
- providing clothing to those who were unable to buy their own
- looking after the sick
- visiting those in prison (vv. 36, 39, 43).

At one point in the parable Jesus says:

*Assuredly, I say to you, inasmuch as you did it to one of the least of these My brethren, you did to Me.* (Matthew 25.40 NKJV)

Thus once again, we see that doing good is part of the Christian life. Not only that; it is also plain that there are serious consequences for those who do *not* do such things (vv. 41–46).

These words of Jesus, however, are rarely discussed in the modern Church, probably because society has changed and people are now uncomfortable with the idea of God judging anyone. This means that many Christians do not seem to realise that whilst we will be judged on our works and rewarded according to what we have done (1 Corinthians 3:10–15), those who do not personally know Christ will not be with us in heaven; theirs is a very different destiny (Revelation 20:15).

God has entrusted the good news of the Kingdom to us – to His children – and we have not just the responsibility to pass it on to those who have not yet been adopted into His family, but also the privilege of doing so.

I have always found a joy in doing so, both in word and deed, as it is so exciting when someone reaches the point of wanting to make a commitment to Christ. Being the 'midwife' in such moments is an incredibly special experience and one that I hope I will have the pleasure of experiencing on many more occasions before eventually going to be with the Lord!

Basically, if we truly love God we will love others too; loving others is not just to be expressed in what we say but also in what we do. This is what the heart of the gospel is all about and is why churches should be involved in social action projects – they are a practical expression of the love of Christ in action as well as being a witness to the way in which He has changed our lives.

I say this because it is recognised that the volunteers working for such projects have made a sacrifice to do what they are doing and, more than that, when such volunteers are all Christians they relate in a different way from those who are not; their concern and care for each other comes across to those whom they are serving, as well as to others who see their service to the community.

Such community projects can serve another purpose, namely that of bringing together Christians from different denominations and streams. This will provide an even stronger witness to the community of the reality of God and of our faith.

Not only that; it will also contribute to bringing down the barriers between Christians from different churches. This brings about greater unity in the Body of Christ within the area involved, something that is essential for helping the life of the Kingdom to multiply more fully.

Returning to the subject of reaching people with the gospel, another thing that churches need to do is to ensure that when new people come into the church they are made welcome. There also needs to be a strategy of some kind in place to enable them to be integrated into community life, because otherwise people will come in the front door, only to go out through the back.

Such a strategy needs to be relational, rather than organisational, so that those who are new to the church feel loved. It needs to include foundational Biblical teaching and basic discipleship, but also to be social, enabling the building of relationships with other members of the congregation.

As I bring this book to a close, I would like to hope that I have underpinned, perhaps even expanded, your understanding not only of the Church and what our life as a community should look like, but also of God and His Kingdom. More than that, I hope that your desire for God will have increased and that therefore you are wanting to discover His heart for you more now than you did previously.

I would love to hear what impact this book has had on your spiritual life, if any, so feel free to contact me through the email address below:

JETthepilgrim@gmail.com

# BOOKS THAT I HAVE FOUND HELPFUL

The Father Heart of God
*Margaret Sylvester, Sovereign World 2012*

The Father You Have Been Waiting For
*Mark Stibbe, Authentic 2005*

The Pleasures of Loving God
*Mike Bickle, Creation House 2000*

The Grace of Yielding
*Derek Prince, Whittaker House*

Intercessor
*Rees Howells, Normam Grubb, The Lutterworth Press 1952*

Shaping History through Prayer and Fasting
*Derek Prince, Whittaker House 1973*

Watchman Prayer
*Dutch Sheets, Regal 2000*